ASL ~ ENGLISH GRAMMAR

A Comparative Linguistics Handbook

Kevin Struxness

Virginia (Ginger) Marable

Thirteenth Edition, Fall 2012

WhitMar Electronic Press, San Diego

ii

Kevin Struxness, MA
Ginger Marable, PhD

WhitMar Electronic Press
San Diego, CA

DEDICATION

In Loving Memory

Beloved Mother
Delores Marston Struxness
1934 - 2012

The authors affectionately dedicate this *Handbook* to anyone who seeks to understand and appreciate the complex beauty of American Sign Language and English.

KS & GM

"The wise accumulate knowledge—a true treasure! . . . The speech/ [signing] of a good person is worth waiting for; [it is] rich fare for many . . . a fountain of wisdom . . . and it clears the air!" (Proverbs 10:14, 21, 31, 32)

CONTENTS

ACKNOWLEDGMENTS x

INTRODUCTION xi

HOW to USE THIS BOOK xii

OVERVIEW of GRAMMAR xiv

ASL GLOSS USED in THIS *HANDBOOK* xvii

SECTION ONE: PARTS of SPEECH 1

Nouns 1
Proper Nouns: Names, Places 1
Proper Nouns: Direct Address 1
Plurality 2
    Ranking 3
    Quantifiers 3
    Cluster Affixes 3
    Demonstrative Pronouns 3
    Reduplication/Repetition 4
    Plural Pronouns 4
    Classifiers 4
    Fingerspelled Words with /-s/ 5
    Adjectives and Verbs 5
Count ~ Non-Count 6
Determiners 6
Possessive Case 7
Agentive Noun Suffixes 8
Nouns Functioning as Adjectives 9

Pronouns 9
Personal 10
    Agreement 10
    Nominative 10
    Objective 10
    Possessive 11
    Adjective/Noun Functions 11

Reflexive *11*
Intensive *12*
Untriggered *13*
Interrogative *13*
Relative *14*
Demonstrative *14*
Double *15*
Indefinite *15*
Reciprocal *16*

Adjectives *17*
   Determiners *17*
   Articles *18*
      Indefinite *18*
      Definite *19*
   Comparatives/Superlatives *20*

Verbs *21*
   Verb Types *21*
      Transitive *22*
      Intransitive *22*
      Linking *22*
      Sensory *22*
         "To Be" *22*
         "To Become" *22*
      ASL Inflected *24*
         Continuous *24*
         Repeated *24*
   Infinitives *24*
   Auxiliary Verbs *25*
      "To Be" *25*
      "To Have" *26*
      "To Do" *26*
      Fingerspelled "Did" *27*
      Modals *27*
      "Used To" *28*
   Verb Tenses *28*
      Simple Present *28*
      Simple Past *29*
         Present Tense as Past Tense *30*
         Change in Mouth Movement *30*
      Future *30*
      Perfect *31*
         Present Perfect *32*
         Past Perfect *32*
         Future Perfect *32*

Conditional Perfect *33*
Progressive/Continuous *33*
Participles *34*
    Gerunds *34*
    Present and Past *35*
Contractions *35*
Directional/Partial-Directional/Non-Directional *36, 37*
Noun-Verb Pairs with a Change in Movement *37*
Noun-Verb Pairs with No Change in Movement *39*
Active ~ Passive Voice *40*

Adverbs *41*
    Manner *42*
    Comparatives/Superlatives *42*
    Intensifiers *43*
    Negation *44*
    Frequency *46*
    Clock Time *46*
    Early, Mid-, Late *47*
    Introductory Adverbial Time/Tense Indicators *47*

Conjunctions *49*
    Coordinating *49*
    Correlative *51*
        Both . . . and . . . *51*
        Not only . . . but also . . . *52*
        Either . . . or . . . *52*
        Neither . . . nor . . . *52*

Prepositions *53*

Interjections *53*

SECTION TWO: SYNTAX (PHRASE and CLAUSE STRUCTURES) *56*

Phrases *56*
    Noun *56*
    Verb *57*
    Infinitive *57*
    Adjective and Adverb *58*
    Prepositional *58*

Declarative Sentence Structures

Basic English Sentence Patterns *58*
- **S Vi** *59*
- **S Vt DO** *59*
- **S Vt IO DO** *59*
- **S Vbe PN** *60*
- **S LV PA** *60*
  - **"There" Vbe S Adv** *61*

Affirmative *62*
Exclamatory *62*
Topicalization (Topic-Comment, etc.) *63*

Interrogative Sentence Structures *63*

Yes/No Questions *63*
Wh- Questions *64*
Rhetorical Questions *67*
Tag Questions *68*

Dependent Clauses *69*

Noun Clauses *69*
Adjectival Clauses *70*
Adverbial Clauses *70*
- **Conditional** *71*
- **Time** *72*

SECTION THREE: LEXICALIZED STRUCTURES *73*

Fingerspelling *73*

Numbers *73*
- **Cardinal Numbers** *73*
- **Ordinal Numbers** *73*
- **"Rule of 9"** *73*

Years *74*
Months of the Year *75*
Age *75*
Height *75*
Abbreviations *75*
Loan Signs *76*
Fingerspelled "It" *78*

Vocabulary *78*

Compound Words *78*
Prefixes *79*
Idiomatic Equivalencies *80*

ASL Abbreviations and Acronyms *91*
U.S. States, ASL Abbreviations *101*

Classifiers *102*
Description: Shape, Size, Texture, Amount and Length *103*
Location: Near and Far; Left and Right; Front and Back *106*
Movement: Stationary, Speed and Direction *108*
Orientation: Arrangement of Objects or Persons *108*
Pluralization: Singular or Plural *109*

SECTION FOUR: NON-MANUAL BEHAVIORS *111*

Grammatical Facial Expressions *111*
Affirmation *111*
Negation *111*
Yes-No Questions *112*
Wh- Questions *112*
Rhetorical Questions *113*
Topic Marker (Topicalization) *113*
Time Marker *113*
Conditional Clauses *114*

Mouth Morphemes *114*
Beginning Level *115*
Beginning-Intermediate Level *118*
Intermediate Level *121*
Advanced Level *129*

SECTION FIVE: STUDY QUESTIONS *129*

Beginning Level *129*
Part A *129*
Part B *133*

Beginning-Intermediate Level *136*
Part A *136*
Part B *139*

Intermediate Level *142*
Part A *142*
Part B *146*

Advanced Level *151*
    Part A *151*
    Part B *156*

Keys for Study Questions *159*

Beginning Level *159*
    Part A *159*
    Part B *163*

Beginning-Intermediate Level *167*
    Part A *167*
    Part B *169*

Intermediate Level *173*
    Part A *173*
    Part B *178*

Advanced Level *184*
    Part A *184*
    Part B *189*

FROM YOUR AUTHORS *194*

ACKNOWLEDGMENTS

The authors would like to express their heartfelt appreciation to the following persons who have so graciously shared their professional and personal expertise in the preparation of this *Handbook*:

Dr. Elizabeth (Liz) Mendoza, instructor in the Interpreter Training Program of Palomar College and author of *ABC 1-2-3 Fingerspelling etc.* (2006)—for her assistance with the Loan Signs section and permission for inclusion of information from Robbin Battison's *Lexical Borrowing in American Sign Language* (1978).

Ashley Iosbaker, Palomar College ASL IV student, for her assistance with copyediting. Rebecca Coleman, graduate of the Palomar College ASL/English Interpreter Training Program, for her suggestions.

Melinda Finn, Palomar College Photographer/Communications Specialist, for the cover photographs of the authors.

Our wonderful American Sign Language students over the past four years at all levels—for their candid commentaries, continual support, and loving encouragement to us, their grateful teachers! This is for you!

KS & GM

Additional resources consulted for this *Handbook* that may be of further interest to the reader include:

Tom Humphries and Carol Padden. (2004). *Learning American Sign Language: Levels 1 & 2, Beginning and Intermediate* (2nd edn.). Boston: Pearson Education.

Edward Klima and Ursula Bellugi. (1979). *The Signs of Language.* Cambridge, MA: Harvard University Press.

William Stokoe, Dorothy Casterline and Carl Croneberg. (1965). *A Dictionary of American Sign Language on Linguistic Principles.* Washington, DC: Gallaudet College Press.

Kevin Struxness. (1996). *Mouth Morphemes in American Sign Language* videotape/DVD. Rio Rancho, NM: DeBee Communications.

Clayton Valli and Ceil Lucas, *Linguistics of American Sign Language: A Resource Text for ASL Users.* (2002). Washington, DC: Gallaudet University Press.

INTRODUCTION

Linguistics is the study of the patterns or structures of a language, including *phonology, morphology, syntax* and *semantics.* For one's first language, or "mother tongue," these patterns are already embedded in the language center of the brain from observation and mimicry in infancy; actually, very young children can learn several different languages simultaneously with native fluency and without an "accent." But for the second, or "foreign" language learner, the linguistics of the target language must be compared to and contrasted with the native language, then practiced repetitively <u>with understanding</u> to achieve any degree of fluency. When one begins to <u>dream</u> in the target language, enough is coming into the language center to form the new patterns and make them ready for automatic retrieval. When one can <u>think</u> in the target language, without translating from the native language, fluency is being achieved.

Phonology, from the Greek root for "sound," is the study of the sound system of a spoken language. *Phonemes* are the smallest sounds that make a contrastive difference in meaning:

> "<u>p</u>in" is distinguished from "<u>b</u>in" because the initial consonant sound makes a difference in the meaning of the two words;
> "p<u>i</u>n" is distinguished from "p<u>a</u>n" because the internal vowel sound makes a difference;
> "pi<u>n</u>" is distinguished from "pi<u>t</u>" because the final consonant sound makes a difference.

For ASL, a contrastive element of one or more of the <u>five parameters of a sign</u> makes the difference in meaning: handshape, palm orientation, location, movement, and facial expression:

> BLUE, GREEN, PURPLE and YELLOW differ only in handshape;
> HORSE and RABBIT differ only in palm orientation;
> DRY, UGLY and SUMMER are signed exactly the same except for location;
> MIND and THINK are signed the same except for movement;
> WINTER and COLD differ only in facial expression.

Morphology, from the Greek root for "form," is the study of the smallest segments of a word or sign that make a difference in <u>meaning</u>, such as roots, prefixes, suffixes, possessives, and compounds, as well as non-verbal/non-manual behaviors for both spoken and visual languages. Here are some examples of *phonemes* that work for both English and ASL:

> a) "legal" ~ "<u>il</u>legal
> b) "teach" ~ "teach<u>er</u>"
> c) "worth" ~ "worth<u>less</u>"
> d) "Coco<u>'s</u>" [fs]

e) "book" + "store" ~ "<u>bookstore</u>"
f) "true" ~ "true<u>?</u>"
g) "what" ~ "#what<u>!</u>"

Additionally, ASL uses <u>continuous</u> or <u>repeated</u> motions of a sign to alter the meaning, while English uses /-ing/ and /-ed, -en/ to indicate verb participles, and /-s/ to indicate both noun plurals and third person singular, present tense verbs.

Syntax, from Latin and Greek for "arrange together," incorporates <u>phrase</u>, <u>clause</u> and <u>sentence</u> structures, i.e., groups of words that function together as units. English has noun, adjective, adverb and prepositional phrases; noun, adjective and adverb clauses; and only six basic sentence patterns, the expansion and combination of which make up all the sentences in the language (see "Overview of Grammar," pp. xivff). ASL delineates five different sentence types according to non-manual behaviors: questions, commands, topicalization, affirmation/negation, and conditionals. All of these syntactical structures are addressed in this *Handbook*.

Semantics, from the Greek for "mean," is the study of the meanings of words or signs. For our purposes, we have included the discussion of such lexicalized structures as fingerspelling, loan signs, classifiers, abbreviations/acronyms, and idiomatic equivalencies, as well as non-manual behaviors, such as facial grammar and mouth morphemes.

Your authors do not know of any other full-length book focused exclusively on the lexicon, phonology, morphology and syntax of American Sign Language compared to and contrasted with English. In this *Handbook*, both ASL and English are used in a bilingual approach to aid students in looking at their native language as a bridge to studying and understanding the other language, whether English or ASL. In other words, deaf students whose native language is ASL can benefit from using this *Handbook* to study and understand English, and conversely, native English speakers can use this *Handbook* to analyze and understand ASL. The *Handbook* need not be limited for use in the ASL classroom, but may be helpful in interpreter education programs and deaf education classes as well.

Your authors hope this *ASL ~ English Grammar: A Comparative Linguistics Handbook* will become a well-used reference work in your library.

KS & GM

HOW TO USE THIS *HANDBOOK*

This *Handbook* may be used as the primary textbook for Comparative Linguistics coursework or for research in this field.

It will work successfully as the supplemental textbook for courses in American Sign Language, at any level, as well as for interpreter education programs and Deaf education courses. It can also be used to teach English to deaf students.

With the help of the Table of Contents and the Index, teachers and students can extrapolate appropriate sections of the *Handbook* to integrate with corresponding lessons from the primary textbook, with lectures or with research.

At the end of the *Handbook* are questions and answers covering the book's various grammatical elements. They are divided into A and B sections for each of four language levels: Beginning, Beginning-Intermediate, Intermediate and Advanced. Teachers may assign the questions for class discussion, for homework or for test/quiz preparation.

This *Handbook* has been additionally designed to be used for comparative linguistics research and lectures, as well as for student presentations. Interpreters and other working professionals in the field can read for content or check for answers to questions about grammar and usage.

Finally, the reader will want to keep this *Handbook* handy on your bookshelf to consult often.

OVERVIEW of GRAMMAR

<u>Note</u>: *Adult native speakers/signers of a language know instinctively whether or not a spoken/signed/written utterance is "correct," or at least understandable, because the grammatical patterns have been embedded in the language center of the brain. But to study a <u>new</u> language, the student must be able to discuss the grammatical structures of both the native language and the target language for comparison and contrast. For this discussion, some knowledge of linguistic nomenclature is required. Simplified, grammatical structures fall into the four categories listed below (along with the abbreviations for them as used in this Handbook):*

*the <u>eight parts of speech</u>

*the <u>three forms</u>—word, phrase and clause; each part of speech does not have all of the three forms.

*their <u>functions</u> in the sentence or utterance being analyzed; these vary for each part of speech.

*the <u>six basic sentence patterns</u> of English.

Abbreviations for these structures as used in this Handbook are indicated in brackets [ ]. Explanations with examples are provided throughout this Handbook.

PARTS of SPEECH	FORMS	FUNCTIONS
NOUN [N]	Word/Phr/Cl	Subject [S] Direct Object of the Verb [DO] Indirect Object of the Verb [IO] Predicate Noun [PN] Object of the Preposition [OP] Adjective [Adj]
Possessive Case	/-'s/	N/Adj
	N Phrases [Phr]	S/DO/PN
	N Clauses [Cl]	S/DO/PN/OP

PRONOUN [Pro]	**Word/Phr**	**N Functions**
Personal		**N Functions**
Possessive		**N/Adj Functions**
Relative		**Introduce N/Adj Cl**
	Pro Phr	**N Functions**
ADJECTIVE [Adj]	**Word/Phr/Cl**	**Adj Functions**
Articles [Art]		**Adj Functions**
Determiners [Det]		**Adj Functions**
Comparatives/Superlatives		**Adj Functions**
	Adj Phr	**Adj/Predicate Adj [PA]**
	Adj Cl	**Adj/PA**
VERB [V]	**Word/Phr**	**V Functions**
Infinitives [Inf]	**Inf Phr**	**N/V Functions**
Verb Types		
Intransitive		**Vi**
Transitive		**Vt**
Linking		**LV**
State of Being		
"To Be"		**Vbe**
"To Become"		**Vbe**
Auxiliary Verbs [Aux]	**Word/Phr**	**V Functions**
Participles /-ed, -en/; /-ing/		**Adj**
Gerunds /-ing/		**N Functions**
	Verb Phr	**V Functions**
ADVERB [Adv]	**Word/Phr/Cl**	**Adv Functions**
Intensifiers		**Modify Adj/Adv**
Comparatives/Superlatives		**Adv**
	Adv Phr	**Adv Functions**
	Adv Cl	**Adv Functions**

PREPOSITION [Prep]	Word/Phr	Prep
Adjectival		Adj Functions
Adverbial		Adv Functions
	Prep Phr	Adj/Adv
CONJUNCTION [Conj]	Word	Conj
Coordinating		Join Similar Structures
Correlative (Paired)		Join Parallel Structures
Subordinating		Introduce Adv Cl
INTERJECTION [Intj]	Word/Phr/Cl	Exclamation
	Int Phr	Exclamation
	Int Cl	Exclamatory Cl

THE SIX BASIC SENTENCE PATTERNS of ENGLISH

<u>Note</u>: *Each of these is discussed in detail in this* **Handbook**.

<u>English-ASL Note</u>: *Compared with the intricacies and varieties of ASL syntactical (phrase and clause) structures, English clauses are simple and straight forward. All English sentences are created from only these patterns—generally having been expanded and/or combined:*

A) Subject - Intransitive Verb [S Vi]

B) Subject - Transitive Verb - Direct Object of the Verb [S Vt DO]

C) Subject - Transitive Verb - Indirect Object of the Verb - Direct Object of the Verb [S Vt IO DO]

D) Subject - Verb "To Be" - Predicate Noun [S Vbe PN]

E) Subject - Linking Verb - Predicate Adjective [S LV PA]

F) "There" - Verb "To Be" - Subject - Adverb ["There" S Vbe Adv]

ASL GLOSS USED in THIS *HANDBOOK*

Note: *A visual-spatial language, ASL does not have its own written form. Consequently, linguists, students and teachers of the language find it useful to use a written coded communication system called "gloss" for replicating and discussing ASL signs and non-verbal behaviors. Although there is general agreement about most of the gloss symbols, there is no one definitive system. ASL signs are written in capital letters, as is standard for both ASL and linguistics textbooks. Below are the additional gloss symbols used in this* **Handbook:**

- **CL:B**   *Classifier, handshape B*

- **[fs]**   *Fingerspelled*

- **[ix]**   *Indexed; finger pointed in the appropriate direction: [ix L] = index left*

- **L, R, C**   *Left, right, center*

- **PO**   *Palm orientation:* **PO** *up, inward, etc.*

- **x**   *Time(s); how many times an item is repeated;* **PEANUT BUTTER (lx, lx).**

- **++**   *Sign repeated twice or more:* **TRAVEL++**

- **-**   *More than one English word needed for one ASL sign:* **TWO-OF-US, EVERY-FRIDAY**

- **/**   *Two or more English equivalents for the same ASL sign:* **NEVERTHELESS/ANYWAY/WHATEVER**

- **/ /**   *Sets off mouth morphemes: /cha/; also /-s/ and other linguistic features*

- **#**   *Fingerspelled loan sign:* **#ALL, #CLUB**

- **___**   *Targeted linguistic structure: fast, fast<u>er</u>, fast<u>est</u>*

- **( )**   *Explanations:* **PAIN** *(signed at mouth)*

<u>Note</u>: Symbols for ASL linguistic structures incorporating non-manual behaviors—such as raised/furrowed eyebrows, head tilt, eye gaze, and head nodding or shaking—are written <u>above</u> the appropriate glossed text.

---TI---

Time marker: _{----TI-----}
<u>TODAY</u> WE STUDY MUST.

---T---

Topic-Comment: _{--------T-------}
<u>OUR TEST</u> HARD!

---WQ---

Wh- question: _{---------------WQ--------------}
<u>WHO INFORM-YOU</u>?

---RQ---

----RQ-----
Rhetorical question: I LEARN <u>WHERE</u>? ASL LAB.

---CC---

----------------CC--------------
Conditional clause: <u>IF WE STUDY HARD</u>, WE PASS!

---Q---

--------Q-------
Yes/No question: <u>YOU SURE</u>?

---N---

---N---
Negation: I <u>NOT</u> AFRAID.

---Y---

--Y--
Affirmation: <u>YES</u>, I-SAME.

SECTION ONE: PARTS OF SPEECH

NOUNS [N]

*English-ASL Note: **Nouns** name persons, places, things and abstract concepts. They are single words, phrases or clauses. They can function as **Subject [S]**, **Predicate Noun [PN]**, **Direct Object of the Verb [DO]**, **Indirect Object of the Verb [IO]**, **Object of the Preposition [OP]** and **Adjective [Adj]**. (See Overview of Grammar, pp. xivff.)*

Proper Nouns: Names, Places

*ASL Note: **Proper nouns** in ASL are generally fingerspelled [fs]: Ramada Inn [fs], or also commonly glossed, like **R-A-M-A-D-A I-N-N**. Many have their own name signs, such as **Gallaudet** and **Laurent-Clerc**.*

English	ASL
I just met Shawn, a new friend.	RECENT I MEET NEW FRIEND, NAME SHAWN [fs].
Leo Jacobs was a famous deaf educator.	FAMOUS DEAF EDUCATOR FIRST NAME LEO [fs], LAST JACOBS [fs].
The California School for the Deaf at Riverside is more than 50 years old.	RIVERSIDE DEAF-SCHOOL (name sign) MORE THAN OLD-50.

Proper Nouns: Direct Address

*ASL Note: ASL does **not** use a person's name or name sign during direct address.*

English	ASL
Billie, can you see me?	--------------Q---------------- HEY, CAN YOU SEE ME?

Nouns: Plurality [Nsg/Npl]

English Notes: 1) Noun plurals *in English are indicated by the written/enunciated* /-s/, *or* /-es/ *if the word ends in a* <u>sibilant</u> ("s/ch/sh" *family*) *sound.*

English Examples:

cat	cat<u>s</u>
bo<u>x</u>	box<u>es</u>
chur<u>ch</u>	church<u>es</u>
ju<u>dge</u>	judg<u>es</u>
wi<u>sh</u>	wish<u>es</u>

2) *English does not use the possessive* /-'s/ *to form plurals, except for some numbers and letters for clarity:* **Our daughter's** (possessive) **report card was all** <u>A's</u> (*to avoid confusion with the word* "as").

<u>*ASL Notes*</u>: 1) *Often where English prefers the plural, ASL prefers the singular. ASL is always assumed to be singular unless otherwise indicated. ASL also assumes that some situations are always plural so do not need to be rendered plural linguistically.*

English	ASL
How many class<u>es</u> are you taking?	----------------------------WQ--------------------------- HOW-MANY <u>CLASS</u> YOU TAKE-UP?
Jackie and Jamie are going to the movie<u>s</u>.	JACKIE [fs], JAMIE [fs] GO <u>MOVIE</u>.
We want more cracker<u>s</u>.	WE WANT MORE <u>CRACKER</u>.
Do you like animal<u>s</u>?	----------------Q------------- YOU LIKE <u>ANIMAL</u>?
Bring hot dog<u>s</u> to the picnic.	BRING <u>HOT-DOG</u> FOR PICNIC.
Lad<u>ies</u> and gentle<u>men</u>	<u>WOMAN, MAN</u> (tap chest 2x)
Boy<u>s</u> and girl<u>s</u>	<u>BOY, GIRL</u> (1x each)

2) Below is the guide for _intentional emphasis of plurality_ in ASL:
   a) Use a <u>number</u> if known. If the count is three or more, use <u>ranking</u>: On non-dominant 5-hand fingers, point finger by finger starting with the thumb, leaving out AND.

English	ASL
Dale has <u>two</u> ASL poetry book<u>s</u>.	DALE HAVE <u>TWO</u> ASL POEM <u>BOOK</u>.
I have <u>three</u> friend<u>s</u> at school: Toby, Ashley and Sonny.	I HAVE <u>THREE</u> <u>FRIEND</u> THERE DEAF-SCHOOL: 1) TOBY [fs], 2) ASHLEY [fs], 3) SONNY [fs].

b) Use a <u>quantifier</u>, a word that expresses quantity.

ALL (of)/#ALL	ANY	BOTH	EACH (of)	EVERY
FEW	LOTS (of)	MANY	NEITHER	NONE (of)
ONE	PILE	ROW	SEVERAL	SOME (of)

English	ASL
There is a <u>pile</u> of laundry in the garage.	GARAGE HAVE <u>PILE</u> (CL:5) DIRTY CLOTHES.

c) Use a <u>cluster affix</u>, such as CLASS, FAMILY, GROUP, TEAM.

English	ASL
The kid<u>s</u> are outside.	1) KID <u>THEY</u> OUTSIDE. 2) KID <u>GROUP</u> OUTSIDE.

d) Use a plural <u>demonstrative pronoun</u> with index finger, THESE/THOSE.

English	ASL
<u>These</u> hearing dog<u>s</u> came from Canine Companions for Independence.	<u>THESE</u> HEARING DOG FROM CCI.

e) Use <u>reduplication/repetition</u> /++/: Repeat the noun sign <u>twice</u> to the dominant side. Repetition <u>cannot</u> be used with a quantifier or a number.

English	ASL
They need blue bow<u>ls</u>.	THEY NEED BLUE BOWL<u>++</u>.
They need <u>some</u> blue bow<u>ls</u>.	1) THEY NEED <u>SOME</u> BLUE <u>BOWL</u>. 2) THEY NEED BLUE <u>BOWL</u> <u>SOME</u>.
Teens like cool thing<u>s</u>.	YOUNG PEOPLE LIKE COOL <u>THING</u>. (Same movement for singular or plural)
Shop<u>s</u>	SHOP<u>++</u>

<u>*ASL Exceptions:*</u>

Many parent<u>s</u> and child<u>ren</u>	MANY PARENT<u>++</u>, CHILD<u>++</u>,
For year<u>s</u> and year<u>s</u>	YEAR<u>++</u> (stationary position)
Thousand<u>s</u> and thousand<u>s</u> of people	THOUSAND<u>++</u> people (stationary position)

*f) Use a <u>plural pronoun</u> (**WE, ALL-OF-YOU, THEY**).*

English	ASL
<u>We</u> go home weekends but <u>you</u> stay at school.	EVERY WEEKEND <u>WE</u> GO HOME BUT <u>ALL-OF-YOU</u> STAY DEAF-SCHOOL.

g) Use a <u>classifier</u>.

English	ASL
Over there are <u>lots</u> of apple<u>s</u>.	THERE HAVE <u>APPLE</u> (<u>CL:Bent-5 PILE</u>).
Terry saw car<u>s</u> on the lot.	TERRY [fs] SAW CAR (<u>CL:3 move-R</u>).

h) ASL has limited use of final /-s/ for plurality. When /-s/ is used, the word <u>must</u> be fingerspelled, even if there is a sign for the word.

Fingerspelled Words That Can Use /-s/:

ACRE<u>S</u>
BILL<u>S</u>
CHIP<u>S</u> (snack)
DAY<u>S</u> (only when combined with a number)
DRUG<u>S</u> (street)
#HOUR<u>S</u> (loan sign, only when combined with a number)
MILE<u>S</u>
PART<u>S</u> (auto)
SEED<u>S</u>
WEEK<u>S</u> (only when combined with a number)

English	ASL
The farmer needs 100 bags of seed<u>s</u> for every two acre<u>s</u> of land.	FARMER NEED 100 BAG SEED<u>S</u> [fs] FOR EVERY TWO ACRE<u>S</u> [fs].
There's a big difference between prescription drug<u>s</u> and street drug<u>s</u>.	PRESCRIPTION PILL, STREET DRUG<u>S</u> [fs] BIG-DIFFERENCE.
Kelsey must wait two hour<u>s</u> for auto part<u>s</u>.	1) KELSEY [fs] MUST WAIT TWO-HOUR FOR CAR PART<u>S</u> [fs] (regular sign for "two-hour"). 2) KELSEY [fs] MUST WAIT TWO #HOUR<u>S</u> [fs] FOR CAR PART<u>S</u> [fs].

i) Plurality *can also apply to certain* adjectives *and* verbs.

English	ASL
We enjoy <u>different</u> food<u>s</u> [Adj].	WE ENJOY DIFFERENT<u>++</u> FOOD.
I often <u>meet</u> friend<u>s</u> at partie<u>s</u> [V].	I MEET<u>++</u> FRIEND PARTY.
She <u>went</u> to a number of store<u>s</u> [V].	SHE GO<u>++</u>-THERE STORE.

Nouns: Count ~ Non-Count

English-ASL Notes: 1) **Count nouns** *can be enumerated:* **one dog, two dogs, several dogs, many dogs,** *etc.* **Thus, one must determine whether a count noun** *is* **singular or plural. Non-count nouns** *do* **not** *have this distinction.*

2) **Non-count nouns** *generally fall into the following categories:*

<u>Mass nouns</u>: equipment, garbage, homework, jewelry, luggage, money, traffic, etc.

<u>Abstract nouns</u>: advice, courage, hope, joy, love, nature, news, peace, etc.

<u>Academics</u>: art, botany, chemistry, education, logic, math, science, etc.

<u>Activities</u>: aerobics, ballet, chess, exercise, music, tennis, etc.

<u>Beverages and liquids</u>: beer, coffee, juice, lotion, milk, oil, soap, syrup, tea, water, etc.

<u>Emotions</u>: anger, boredom, enthusiasm, fun, happiness, pride, thankfulness, etc.

<u>Gerunds</u>: knitting, painting, singing, skiing, swimming, etc.

<u>Illnesses</u>: apnea, diarrhea, influenza, measles, mumps, sinusitis, etc.

<u>Physical states</u>: exhaustion, health, hunger, starvation, thirst, etc.

3) **Determiners** *for* **count** *and* **non-count nouns** *include the following (* indicates both English and ASL determiner):*

	Count Nouns	**Non-Count Nouns**
<u>Singular</u>	a dollar	*money
	the dollar	the money
	*one dollar	*some money
	*each/every dollar	*a lot/great deal of money
	*another dollar	a/very/too *little money
		*no money
<u>Plural</u>	dollars	*not any money
	*two dollars	*not/too much money
	*some dollars	*(not) enough money
	*several dollars	
	a lot/lots of dollars	
	a great/large number of dollars	
	*no dollars	
	*not any dollars	
	*(not) many dollars	

a/very *few dollars
*(not) enough dollars

English	ASL
Robin asked Channing for <u>five dollars</u>.	ROBIN [fs] ASK CHANNING [fs] <u>FIVE DOLLAR</u> BORROW.
Channing did<u>n't</u> have <u>any money</u>.	CHANNING [fs] HAVE <u>NO MONEY</u>.

Nouns: Possessive Case

<u>English Notes:</u> *The rules for making the possessive case of English nouns are simple but often misunderstood:*

1) Write the target noun, either singular or plural.

2) Add /-'s/.

3) If the word already ends in /-s/, including the plural form, add an apostrophe with <u>no</u> /-s/, symbol /-'Ø/. (Old English made noun plurals by adding /-es/. Hence the apostrophe in Modern English spelling, which indicates that the original /-e/ has been deleted.)

4) If a word ends in /-ss/, the /-'Ø/ is often used to avoid 3 /-s/ in a row.

5) <u>Never add</u> /-s'/, as there is <u>no</u> such pattern in English spelling.

<u>English Examples:</u>

The heel of the shoe = the shoe<u>'s</u> heel
The heels of the shoes = the shoes<u>'</u> heels (/-'Ø/)

The house of Marty Jones = Marty Jones<u>'s</u> house; Marty Jones<u>'</u> house (/-'Ø/)
The house of the Joneses = the Joneses<u>'</u> house (/-'Ø/)

The stem of the glass = the glass<u>'s</u> stem; the glass<u>'</u> stem (/-'Ø/)
The stems of the glasses = the glasses<u>'</u> stems (/-'Ø/)

English	ASL
Driver's license	DRIVE LICENSE
My deaf sister<u>'s</u> name is Brenda.	1) MY DEAF SISTER<u>'S</u> NAME BRENDA [fs].

8

	2) MY DEAF SISTER <u>HER</u> NAME BRENDA [fs].
	3) MY DEAF SISTER NAME BRENDA [fs].
Mother's Day, Lion's Club	MOTHER DAY, LION #CLUB
Valentine's Day	VALENTINE/HEART DAY
Levi's	LEVIS [fs] (no /'/)

ASL Exceptions:

1) Keep the [-'s] in certain proper names: **DENNY<u>'S</u>, CARL<u>'S</u> JR., COCO<u>'S</u>.** *(**ASL Note:** McDonald's has its own name sign variations.)*

2) The possessive personal pronoun "whose" is signed **WHO<u>'S</u>;** *in English, "who's" is the contraction for "who is," as in "Who<u>'s</u> there?"*

English	ASL
<u>Wh</u>ose book is this?	1) <u>WHO'S</u> BOOK THIS?
	2) <u>WHO</u> BOOK BELONG?

Agentive Noun Suffixes

English-ASL Note: *To show that a* noun *represents a person, English often adds agentive suffixes, such as /-er, -or/, /-ant, -ent/, /-an, -ian/ and /-ist/. ASL uses the agentive suffix B:B, palms center, moving downward.*

Examples: **LAWY<u>ER</u>, TEACH<u>ER</u>, WORK<u>ER</u>; GOVERN<u>OR</u>, SENAT<u>OR</u>; DEFEND<u>ANT</u>, STUD<u>ENT</u>; AMERIC<u>AN</u>, MUSIC<u>IAN</u>; ART<u>IST</u>, PIAN<u>IST</u>.**

ASL Exceptions: *1) While English can use* agentive suffixes *for <u>things</u>, ASL cannot.*

English	ASL
There's ice cream in the free<u>zer</u>.	FREEZE++ HAVE ICE CREAM.
I bought a new DVD play<u>er</u> yesterday.	YESTERDAY I BUY NEW DVD <u>MACHINE</u>.
Where are the wash<u>er</u> and dry<u>er</u>?	<u>WASHER</u>, <u>DRYER</u> WHERE? (specific ASL signs)

2) Sometimes English does not use an agent but ASL _must_:

English	ASL
Father is our <u>cook</u> tonight.	TONIGHT FATHER OUR <u>COOK</u>.
Who is our <u>pilot</u>?	---WQ--- OUR <u>PILOT</u> WHO?

Nouns Functioning as Adjectives

<u>English-ASL Note</u>: English and ASL both use nouns in an adjectival function to modify other nouns, unlike many other languages that have to put the adjective <u>after</u> the noun. Spanish and French, for example, must translate "<u>Christmas</u> tree" as "arbol <u>de Navidad</u>" and "bouche <u>de Noel</u>," meaning "tree <u>of Christmas</u>," respectively. (In those languages, the descriptive noun is functioning as the object of the preposition "de," meaning "of.")

<u>English-ASL Examples</u>:

<u>FLOWER</u> GARDEN   <u>OCEAN</u> VIEW   <u>STUDENT</u> HANDBOOK   <u>VEGETABLE</u> SOUP

PRONOUNS [Pro]

<u>English-ASL Note</u>: **Pronouns replace nouns [N]; the noun that a pronoun replaces is its "antecedent." Pronouns can be single words or phrases. The function options for pronouns are the same as for nouns: Subject [S], Predicate Noun [PN], Direct Object of the Verb [DO], Indirect Object of the Verb [IO] and Object of the Preposition [OP].**

<u>English Note</u>: **In English, a pronoun must agree with its antecedent in both <u>number</u> (singular or plural) and <u>gender</u>:**

My sister and brother are twins. <u>They</u> are 10. <u>She</u> is already tall, but <u>he</u> is still short.

<u>ASL Notes</u>: 1) Pronouns are expressed by pointing at a person, place or object.

2) If the person or object is not present, decide where to point and keep the same location as a <u>referent</u> throughout the conversation. This is indicated in the examples below as: [ix R], "indexed right," etc.

English	ASL
Bob was a great guy. I miss <u>him</u>.	1) BOB [fs] <u>HE [ix R]</u> GREAT GUY. I MISS <u>HIM [ix R]</u>. 2) BOB [fs] <u>HE [ix L]</u> GREAT GUY. I MISS <u>HIM [ix L]</u>.

3) Although English requires that the pronoun be restated with each new sentence, ASL does not, as the actor is assumed.

English	ASL
Chocolate is my favorite candy; <u>it</u> is delicious!	CHOCOLATE MY FAVORITE CANDY; DELICIOUS!
<u>We</u>'ve been studying all night; <u>we</u> are burned out.	ALL-NIGHT <u>WE</u> STUDY++; BURNOUT.
Does <u>he</u> have a car? Yes, <u>he</u> does.	------------Q---------- CAR <u>HE</u> HAVE? YES, HAVE CAR.

Pronouns: Personal

<u>English-ASL Note</u>: *The personal pronouns are the same in English and ASL:*

Nominative (Subject, Predicate N)		Objective (Direct Object, Indirect Object, Object of the Preposition)	
Singular	*Plural*	*Singular*	*Plural*
I	we	me	us
you	you	you	you
he, she, it	they	him, her, it	them

<u>ASL Note</u>: *Possessive pronouns are formed with the B handshape.*

Possessive w/Adjective Function		Possessive w/Noun Function	
Singular	*Plural*	*Singular*	*Plural*
MY	OUR	MINE	OURS
YOUR	YOUR	YOURS	YOURS
HIS, HER, ITS	THEIR	HIS, HERS, ITS	THEIRS

English	ASL
That is <u>my</u> hat. [Adj function]	THAT <u>MY</u> (1x) HAT.
That hat is <u>mine</u>. [N function]	THAT HAT <u>MINE</u> (2x).
The key is <u>hers</u>. [N function]	KEY [ix L] <u>HERS</u>. (2x)

English Exception: *There is no third person singular possessive neuter pronoun ("its") with noun function. ASL, however, can express this pronoun because the sign is gender neutral.*

English	ASL
The dog has <u>its</u> toys. [Adj function]	DOG HAVE <u>ITS [ix R]</u> PLAY THING.
The toys are <u>its</u>. (<u>not</u> grammatical English)	PLAY THING <u>ITS [ix R]</u>. (2x)

Pronouns: Reflexive

ASL Notes: *1) Reflexive pronouns are formed with the **Open A** handshape (PO center) and bounced either once or twice.*

2) If the plural refers to <u>two</u> persons only, <u>bounce</u> the hand twice [++] to the side or <u>slide</u> the hand [→] to the side. If <u>more than two</u>, <u>slide</u> the hand.

12

Singular	Plural
MYSELF	OURSELVES
YOURSELF	YOURSELVES
HIMSELF, HERSELF, ITSELF	THEMSELVES

English Notes: *1) Reflexive pronouns* refer back to the subject, or other *antecedent,* and usually function as direct object of the verb [DO] or object of the preposition [OP].

English Examples:

I cut myself. [DO]

When alone, do deaf people sign to themselves? [OP]

2) When the reflexive pronoun follows the preposition "by," the meaning is "alone." The function of this prepositional phrase [Prep Phr] is adverb.

English	ASL
I don't want to study for the ASL test by myself. [Adv Prep Phr]	------------N------------ I DON'T-WANT STUDY FOR ASL TEST ALONE.

English-ASL Note: Reflexives are also used for emphasis and can immediately follow the antecedent; these are sometimes called "intensive" pronouns.

English	ASL
1) The boss himself typed the letter.	1) BOSS HIMSELF-R TYPE LETTER.
2) The boss typed the letter himself.	2) BOSS TYPE LETTER HIMSELF-R.

ASL Notes: *1) Reflexive pronouns* can function as the linking verb "To Be."

English	ASL
Kip and Kerry are codas. (children of deaf adults)	1) KIP [fs], KERRY [fs] THEMSELVES++ CODA [fs].

Are you two DODs? (deaf children of deaf adults)	------------------Q----------------- YOURSELVES++ DOD [fs]?
We're NODAs. (neighbors of deaf adults)	OURSELVES NODA [fs].

2) Reflexive pronouns *also regularly function as* nouns or pronouns.

English	ASL
I like blue, but you prefer red.	MYSELF LIKE BLUE, BUT YOURSELF PREFER RED.

English Note: Beware of the ungrammatical <u>untriggered reflexive</u>*, which is sometimes used instead of the objective personal pronoun in compound phrases.*

English Examples:

Ungrammatical English	Grammatical English
Please wait for Cameron and myself.	Please wait for Cameron and me. [OP]
Myself and Jody are at fault.	Jody and I are at fault. [S]

Pronouns: Interrogative

English-ASL Note: Interrogative pronouns are used to ask questions. They have basically the same form and function in both English and ASL. In the chart below, ASL interrogative pronouns are represented in **CAPITALS.**

how/HOW	how much/HOW-MUCH	how many/HOW-MANY
how often/HOW OFTEN	what/WHAT	when/WHEN
where/WHERE	which/WHICH	who/whom/WHO
whose/WHO'S	why/WHY, FOR-FOR	why not/WHY–NOT

ASL Note: There is no "whom" in ASL; English "whose" is signed **WHO'S.**

Note: For examples of interrogative pronouns *in questions, see* <u>Interrogative Sentence Structures: Wh- Questions</u> *on pp. 64ff.*

Pronouns: Relative

English-ASL Notes: 1) The function of relative pronouns *is to introduce* noun clauses **[NCl]** and adjective clauses **[Adj Cl]**.

2) The relative pronouns *that* introduce **N Cl** and **Adj Cl** *are* "who/whom," "whose," "which" *and* "that." "Who" *refers to people,* "which" *refers to things, and* "that" *can refer to either people or things.* "Whose" *is possessive; ASL signs* **WHO'S.**

3) "Who" *is the nominative case and is used for* subject **[S]** *and* predicate noun **[PN]** *functions;* "whom" *is the objective case in English and is used for* direct object of the verb **[DO]** *and* object of the preposition **[OP]**. *ASL does not have* "whom."

ASL Note: **Relative pronouns** *in ASL require no grammatical facial expression.*

English	ASL
I believe <u>that</u> they are deaf. [N Cl as DO]	I BELIEVE THEY DEAF.
Marlee Matlin is the deaf actor <u>who</u> won an Oscar. [S of Adj Cl]	MARLEE MATLIN [fs] DEAF ACTOR <u>WHO</u> WIN OSCAR [fs].
The theater in Los Angeles <u>that</u> offers signed drama is Deaf West Theatre. [S of Adj Cl]	THEATER THERE LA OFFER ASL PERFORMANCE NAME DEAF WEST THEATRE [fs].
Pat is the ASL instructor <u>whom</u> I admire the most. [DO of Adj Cl]	--T-- 1) PAT [fs] THAT-ONE ASL TEACHER I RESPECT MOST. --T-- 2) PAT [fs] ASL TEACHER THAT-ONE I RESPECT MOST.

Pronouns: Demonstrative

English-ASL Note: The demonstrative pronouns *are used to* "point out" *nouns:* "this"/"that" *in the singular and* "these"/"those" *in the plural.*

English	ASL
For pagers, I like <u>these</u> but not <u>those</u>.	PAGER, <u>THESE</u> I LIKE, <u>THOSE</u> NOT-LIKE.
<u>This one</u> is good, but <u>that one</u> is awesome!	<u>THIS</u> GOOD, <u>THAT-ONE</u> AWESOME!

Pronouns: Double

ASL Note: 1) Single pronouns are perfectly all right.

2) Don't mouth the <u>subject</u> pronoun <u>occurring or repeated at the end</u> of a sentence. Mouthing subject pronouns at the <u>beginning</u> of a sentence and <u>object</u> pronouns <u>after the verb</u> is appropriate.

English	ASL
<u>I</u> love CSDR!	<u>I</u> KISS-FIST RIVERSIDE DEAF-SCHOOL <u>I</u>! (no mouthing second "I")
Are <u>they</u> taking ASL?	----------------------Q--------------------- <u>THEY</u> TAKE-UP ASL <u>THEY</u>? (no mouthing second "THEY")
Are <u>you</u> deaf?	---------Q-------- DEAF <u>YOU</u>? (no mouthing "YOU")
<u>She</u> told <u>me</u>,	<u>SHE</u> TOLD <u>ME</u>. (mouth both subject and object pronouns)

Pronouns: Indefinite

English-ASL Note: The indefinite pronouns do not substitute for nouns, but function themselves as <u>singular</u> nouns.

ANY	ANYBODY/ANYONE	EACH (of)
EVERYBODY/EVERYONE	PEOPLE ALL-OVER	NOBODY/NO ONE
NONE (of)	SOMEBODY/SOMEONE	

English	ASL
<u>Everybody</u> needs <u>someone</u>.	<u>EVERY-ONE</u> NEED <u>SOMEONE</u>. [S, DO]
<u>Nobody</u> wants <u>anything</u> to eat.	<u>NO ONE</u> WANT EAT <u>ANYTHING</u>. [S, DO]
<u>Each of</u> the deaf mainstreamed children has an interpreter.	DEAF MAINSTREAM CHILD++, <u>EACH++</u> HAVE INTERPRETER. [S]

<u>ASL Note</u>: ASL does <u>not</u> have the singular indefinite pronoun "one."

English	ASL
Chris sold two cars and bought a new <u>one</u>.	CHRIS SOLD TWO CAR AND BUY NEW CAR.
I have two cookies; do you want <u>one</u>?	I HAVE TWO COOKIE; 1) YOU WANT? 2) YOU WANT POINT [ix cookie]?

Pronouns: Reciprocal

<u>English-ASL Note</u>: The reciprocal pronouns are "each other" and "one another." They are used interchangeably in English and share the same sign in ASL.

English	ASL
Sweethearts often buy gifts for <u>each other</u>.	SWEETHEART OFTEN BUY GIFT FOR <u>EACH-OTHER</u>.
Let's respect <u>one another</u>.	1) LET RESPECT <u>EACH-OTHER</u>. 2) LET TWO-OF-US RESPECT <u>EACH-OTHER</u>.

Adjectives [Adj]

<u>English Notes</u>: 1) Adjectives [Adj] modify nouns [N]. In English they generally <u>precede</u> the noun they are describing. There are specific word order patterns for English adjectives:

2) <u>article/determiner [Art/Det]</u> → <u>opinion</u> → <u>fact</u> → N

English Examples:

<u>our</u> <u>favorite</u> <u>ASL</u> DVD

<u>that</u> <u>delicious</u> <u>homemade</u> burrito

    3) <u>Art/Det</u> → <u>size</u> → <u>age</u> → <u>color</u> → <u>origin/source</u> → <u>material</u> → N

English Examples:

<u>the</u> <u>enormous</u> <u>new</u> <u>silver</u> <u>imported</u> <u>hybrid</u> minivan

<u>six</u> <u>young</u> <u>golden retriever</u> <u>hearing</u> dogs

ASL Notes: *1) An ASL adjective can sometimes be placed <u>before</u> or <u>after</u> a noun, or <u>both</u> for emphasis or excitement.*

English	ASL
We are eating a <u>hot</u> meal.	1) WE EAT <u>HOT</u> MEAL. 2) WE EAT MEAL <u>HOT</u>. 3) WE EAT <u>HOT</u> MEAL <u>HOT</u>.
They love the <u>cool</u> videophone.	1) THEY KISS-FIST <u>COOL</u> VP. 2) THEY KISS-FIST VP <u>COOL</u>. 3) THEY KISS-FIST <u>COOL</u> VP <u>COOL</u>.

2) If three or more adjectives, place all <u>after</u> the noun.

English	ASL
I hate <u>long</u>, <u>boring</u>, <u>old</u> movies.	MOVIE <u>LONG, BORE, OLD</u>, I YUCK.
My family loves <u>warm, fresh organic</u> peach pie.	MY FAMILY KISS-FIST PEACH PIE <u>WARM, FRESH, ORGANIC</u> [fs].

3) Sometimes an adjective can be signed <u>twice</u>, rather than once, if the adjective is placed <u>after</u> the noun.

English	ASL
Darryl has a <u>red</u> hearing-aid mold.	DARRYL [fs] HAVE <u>RED</u> [1x] HEARING-AID MOLD.

Shelly bought a <u>new</u> car.	1) SHELLY [fs] BUY <u>NEW</u> CAR. [1x] 2) SHELLY [fs] BUY CAR <u>NEW</u>. [1x or 2x] 3) SHELLY [fs] BUY <u>NEW</u> CAR <u>NEW</u>. [1x, 1x]
We enjoy <u>different</u> places.	1) WE ENJOY <u>DIFFERENT++</u> PLACE. 2) WE ENJOY PLACE <u>DIFFERENT++</u>.
They have <u>enough</u> time.	THEY HAVE <u>ENOUGH</u> TIME. [1x]
That's <u>enough</u>.	<u>ENOUGH</u>. [2x]
ASL is a <u>hard</u> class.	1) ASL <u>HARD</u> CLASS. [1x] 2) ASL CLASS <u>HARD</u>. [1x or 2x]

Adjectives: Determiners

English-ASL Note: *"Determiners" are various markers for nouns. They include* <u>*articles*</u>*,* <u>*possessive pronouns*</u>*,* <u>*demonstrative pronouns*</u>*,* <u>*quantifiers*</u> *and* <u>*numbers*</u>*. (All are discussed in this* **Handbook***.)*

Adjectives: Articles

English Notes: **Articles** *are used* <u>*before*</u> **English** *nouns.*

> *1) The* <u>*indefinite*</u> *article "a" (or its variant "an," which is used before a word beginning with a vowel) indicates* <u>*any*</u> *general,* <u>*nonspecific*</u> *noun. Its plural forms are "some" and /Ø/ (no article present).*

English Examples:

Singular	Plural
I'd like <u>a</u> banana and <u>an</u> orange.	1) I'd like <u>some</u> banana<u>s</u> and <u>some</u> orange<u>s</u>. 2) I'd like <u>some</u> banana<u>s</u> and /<u>Ø</u>/ orange<u>s</u>. 3) I'd like /<u>Ø</u>/ banana<u>s</u> and /<u>Ø</u>/ orange<u>s</u>.

> *2) The* <u>*definite*</u> *article "the" indicates a* <u>*specific*</u> *noun. Its plural form is also "the."*

English Example:

Singular

Did <u>the</u> light flash on <u>the</u> TTY?

Plural

Did <u>the</u> light<u>s</u> flash on <u>the</u> TTY<u>s</u>?

ASL Notes: 1) *ASL does not generally use "a"/"an"/"some" (indefinite) or "the" (definite). Seldom keep "the" for specifying a person or an object, especially in the presence of the signer.*

English	ASL
I have <u>the</u> videophone equipment.	I HAVE VP EQUIPMENT.
Do you own <u>a</u> pager?	---------------Q--------------- YOU HAVE PAGER?
They work five days <u>a</u> week.	THEY WORK FIVE-DAY <u>EVERY-WEEK</u>.

ASL Exceptions:

1) In ASL, the definite article "the" is expressed by pointing with an index finger to an object or person, especially in the presence of the signer.

English	ASL
<u>The</u> car needs some repairs.	1) <u>POINT [ix R]</u> CAR NEED FIX. 2) CAR <u>POINT [ix R]</u> NEED FIX.
<u>The</u> dog is smart.	1) <u>POINT [ix L]</u> DOG SMART. 2) DOG <u>POINT [ix L]</u> SMART. 3) DOG SMART <u>POINT [ix L]</u>.

2) Keep the article if it is part of a title or name: "<u>A</u> Girl Called Alice," Georgia School for <u>the</u> Deaf.

2) With comparative numbers, ASL uses #<u>OR UP/MINIMUM</u> to express larger numbers, such as English "100 or <u>higher</u>," "120 degrees or <u>hotter</u>" and "age 21 or <u>older</u>."

English	ASL
To play sports, students must have a GPA of 2.0 or <u>higher</u>.	STUDENT MUST HAVE GPA 2.0 <u>#OR MINIMUM</u> PLAY SPORT.

Free admission for kids 5 <u>and under</u>. FREE ADMISSION FOR KID AGE 5 <u>#OR BELOW</u>.

Adjectives: Comparatives/Superlatives

English-ASL Notes: 1) The comparative and superlative forms of adjectives [Adj] are used to compare two or more nouns [N].

2) For the <u>equivalent</u> comparison of an adjective, use [<u>as</u> (Adj) <u>as</u> (N)].

3) For the English <u>comparative</u> form of an Adj, add [<u>-er than</u>] to the Adj.

4) For the English <u>superlative</u> form of an Adj, add [<u>the</u> (Adj) <u>-est</u>] (<u>of all</u>).

English Examples:

Equal: My twin brother is just <u>as</u> old <u>as</u> I am.

Comparative: Our sister is old<u>er than</u> either of us.

Superlative: Our baby brother is <u>the</u> young<u>est</u> <u>of all</u> of us.

5) If the English adjective is long, use [<u>more/less</u> (Adj) <u>than</u>] and [<u>the most/least</u> (Adj) (<u>of all</u>)].

English Examples:

Tennies are <u>more</u> comfortable <u>than</u> high heels, but sandals are <u>the most</u> comfortable.

NTID is <u>less</u> expensive <u>than</u> Gallaudet, but CSUN is <u>the least</u> expensive <u>of all</u>.

ASL Notes: 1) ASL has the same three levels of comparison plus several other options, including /"shot H"/ and <u>setting up in space</u> the items to be compared.

2) MORE/LESS THAN can be used with <u>any</u> adjective sign.

3) The sign shot H means "beat," "win," "defeat," "vanquish." It is made with handshape S>H, directional from victor to vanquished. Mouth /po/.

English	ASL
A gorilla is lar<u>ger than</u> a monkey.	1) GORILLA <u>LARGER THAN</u> MONKEY. 2) GORILLA <u>MORE LARGE THAN</u> MONKEY. 3) FOR BODY SIZE, GORILLA <u>BEAT</u> /shot H/ MONKEY. -------------T------------- ------------T------------ 4) GORILLA [ix L], MONKEY [ix R]; <u>LARGER, POINT [ix L]</u>.

4) For [-er] and [-est], ASL adds the open A *handshape* to *the adjective, bringing the affix up higher for* [-est].

Shaq was not <u>the</u> tall<u>est</u> player in the NBA.	BEFORE SHAQ [fs] NOT TALL<u>EST</u> PLAYER NBA.

VERBS [V]

Verb Types

<u>Note:</u> **Verbs *can be either single words or phrases. They function as noted directly below.***

<u>English Notes:</u> *There are three types of verbs in English,* <u>transitive</u> **[Vt],** <u>intransitive</u> **[Vi],** *and* <u>linking</u> **[LV].**

   1) A transitive verb moves the action from the subject **[S]** *to the direct object of the verb* **[DO].**

<u>English Examples:</u>

Mack [S] <u>bit</u> Jack [DO], then Jack [S] <u>hit</u> Mack [DO].

   2) An intransitive verb does not transfer any action; there is no object. **Intransitive verbs *function the same in English and ASL.***

English	ASL
Babies <u>cry</u>.	BABY <u>CRY</u>.
Fish <u>swim</u>.	FISH <u>SWIM</u>.

3) One type of linking verb is <u>sensory verbs</u>: "appear," "feel," "look," "smell," "sound like," "taste," "seem," etc. They are usually followed by a predicate adjective [PA] describing the subject.

English Examples:

This fish <u>looks</u> and <u>feels</u> slimy [PA], and <u>smells</u> and <u>tastes</u> disgusting [PA]! It <u>seems</u> spoiled [PA].

4) Another type of linking verb is state of being verbs [Vbe]: "be" and "become." They are usually followed by either a predicate adjective [PA] or a predicate noun [PN].

English Examples:

Dr. Robert Davila <u>became</u> President [PN] of Gallaudet. He <u>had been</u> Vice-President [PN] of RIT and CEO [PN] of NTID.

ASL Notes: 1) "To Become" functions regularly in ASL.

English	ASL
Marty <u>became</u> sick. [PA]	MARTY [fs] <u>FINISH</u> BECOME SICK.
Taylor wants <u>to become</u> secretary of the National Association of the Deaf. [PN]	TAYLOR [fs] WANT <u>BECOME</u> SECRETARY FOR NAD.

2) There is no "To Be" in ASL:

English	ASL
That captioned movie <u>was</u> great!	CAPTION MOVIE THUMB-UP++.
I <u>am</u> so happy!	I HAPPY I!

ASL Exceptions:

1) CAN'T <u>BE</u> [fs].

2) **Reflexive pronouns** *can function as* **linking verbs:**

English	ASL
Shannon and Toby <u>are</u> ASL students.	SHANNON [fs], TOBY [fs] <u>THEMSELVES++</u> ASL STUDENT.
I'<u>m</u> the new captain of our soccer team.	I <u>MYSELF</u> NEW CAPTAIN OUR SOCCER TEAM.

3) Use sign PAST/BEFORE *for the past tense of* "To Be": "was/were/have been," *etc.*

English	ASL
Leroy <u>was</u> only a box boy; now he is the manager.	<u>BEFORE</u> LEROY [fs] JUST BOX BOY; NOW MANAGER.
There <u>used to be</u> six owls at the zoo.	<u>PAST</u> ZOO [fs] HAVE SIX OWL.

4) Use sign FUTURE/WILL *for* "will be."

English	ASL
The new road <u>will be</u> open in July.	----------TI---------- <u>FUTURE JULY</u> NEW ROAD READY.
Markey <u>will be</u> introducing the speaker.	MARKEY [fs] INTRODOUCE SPEAKER <u>WILL</u>.

5) Use sign NOW/PRESENT *for* "am/is/are/being."

English	ASL
The turtles <u>are being</u> released into the bay.	<u>NOW</u> TURTLE THEY FREE THERE BAY [fs].
The Disneyland entrance gate <u>is</u> closed.	ENTRANCE GATE THERE DISNEYLAND <u>NOW</u> CLOSED.

<u>*English-ASL Note:*</u> *Like English, all ASL clauses need a <u>subject</u>, meaning the main noun and its modifiers, and a <u>predicate</u>, meaning the verb, its modifiers and everything else in the sentence.*

<u>*English-ASL Exceptions:*</u> *The subject and/or verb might be omitted when understood:* **WHERE? YOUR NAME? WHAT TIME?**

6) ASL <u>inflected verbs</u> *alter the meaning of the signed verb by repeating the movement of the sign.* Verbs *that indicate a <u>continuous</u>, non-stop action are*

signed over and over in a circular manner. **Verbs** *that indicate a* <u>repeated</u>*, from time-to-time action are signed over and over with a pause in between.*

English	ASL
Our creek <u>keeps running</u> day in and and day out, all year around.	OUR SMALL RIVER <u>FLOW-CONTINUOUS</u> ALL-DAY, ALL-NIGHT YEAR-ROUND.
That old clock <u>works non-stop</u> 24 hours a day.	OLD CLOCK THAT-ONE <u>CONTINUE-CONTINUOUS</u>, NEVER STOP 24 HOUR EVERYDAY.
The 7-11 has customers <u>coming and going</u>, especially on weekends.	7-11 STORE FAMOUS FOR CUSTOMER <u>ENTER-EXIT-CONTINUOUS</u>, WORSE EVERY WEEKEND.
Grandmother <u>sends</u> a <u>weekly</u> letter of opinion to the newspaper.	----------T---------- NEWSPAPER GRANDMOTHER <u>SEND-REPEATED</u> HER OPINION EVERY-WEEK.
My wife and I have been going to the state fair since 1985.	EVERY-YEAR SINCE 1985, MY WIFE TWO-OF-US <u>GO-REPEAT</u> STATE FAIR.
At nighttime, owl parents keep busy <u>bringing</u> rodents for their owlets.	DURING NIGHT, OWL PARENT++ BUSY <u>BRING-REPEATED</u> MOUSE FOR BABY OWL.

Verbs: Infinitives

<u>*English Notes:*</u> *1) The* <u>infinitive</u>*, or* <u>base</u> *form, of a verb is the* <u>unconjugated</u> *form, meaning it does not have* <u>person</u> *(first, second, third),* <u>number</u> *(singular or plural) or* <u>tense</u>*. Its marker is "to":* "<u>to</u> jump," "<u>to</u> love," "<u>to</u> be."

2) See the **Infinitive Phrases** *section on p. 57.*

<u>*ASL Notes:*</u> *1) ASL does* <u>not</u> *have an infinitive marker ["to"].*

2) Delete the "to" infinitive marker in combination with a verb.

English	ASL
We <u>need to complete</u> the task.	WE <u>NEED</u> <u>FINISH</u> JOB.

The kids <u>want to play</u>.	THEY KID <u>WANT</u> <u>PLAY</u>.
Our ASL students <u>love to sign</u>.	OUR ASL STUDENT <u>KISS-FIST</u> <u>SIGN</u>.

Auxiliary Verbs [Aux]

English Notes: 1) An auxiliary is used with a verb to indicate tense. English has five types of auxiliaries: "To Be," "To Have," "To Do," Modals and "Used To."

2) English loves "To Be," "To Have" and "To Do" so much that they are used as verbs in their own right as well as auxiliaries. Because they have been used so often through the ages, they have remained irregular in form.

Auxiliary Verb: "To Be"

English Note: The auxiliary "To Be" is used to make progressive/continuous tenses [Cont t] (discussed in detail on p. 33). It is <u>not</u> the same as the linking verb [Vbe] (discussed on p. 22).

ASL Note: Remember, there is <u>no</u> "To Be" in ASL.

English	ASL
She <u>is</u> an interpreter, right? [S Vbe PN] No, she <u>is</u> work<u>ing</u> here as a substitute ASL teacher. [Pres Cont t]	SHE INTERPRETER, RIGHT? NO, SHE WORK HERE SUBSTITUTE ASL TEACHER.
I <u>am</u> read<u>ing</u>. [Pres Cont t]	1) I NOW READ. 2) I READ++.
The dog <u>has been</u> sleep<u>ing</u>. [Pres perf Cont t]	1) DOG SLEEP SINCE. 2) DOG SLEEP-CONTINUOUS (continuous motion)

Auxiliary Verb: "To Have"

English-ASL Notes: 1) The auxiliary "To Have" is used to make perfect tenses. It is <u>not</u> the same as the transitive verb [Vt].

2) The transitive verb "To Have" in both English and ASL is used for two purposes—possession and existence.

English	ASL
The office <u>has</u> five chairs. (possession)	OFFICE THERE <u>HAVE</u> FIVE CHAIR. [S Vt DO]
Sears <u>has</u> power tools. (existence)	SEARS [fs] <u>HAVE</u> ELECTRIC TOOL [fs]. [S Vt DO]

3) The English auxiliary in perfect tenses ["To Have" + V + Past Participle /-ed, -en/] is signed "FINISH." (Perfect tense is discussed in detail on p. 32.)

English	ASL
The two professors <u>have written</u> a book. [Pres Perf t]	1) TWO PROFESSOR <u>WRITE</u> BOOK <u>FINISH</u>. 2) TWO PROFESSOR <u>FINISH WRITE</u> BOOK.

Auxiliary Verb: "To Do"

<u>English Note:</u> *The auxiliary [Aux] "To Do" is used for questions and negatives/affirmatives where there is <u>no other</u> auxiliary or the verb "to be" [Vbe]. It is <u>not</u> the same as the transitive verb [Vt] "to do," meaning "to act."*

English	ASL
We always <u>do</u> our homework. [S <u>Vt</u> DO]	WE ALWAYS <u>DO</u> OUR HOMEWORK.
<u>Do</u> you <u>sign</u>? [question Aux]	--------Q-------- YOU SIGN?
Yes, I <u>do</u>. [affirmative)]	--Y-- <u>YES</u>, I SIGN.
No, I <u>don't</u>. [negative]	-------------N------------- <u>NO, I NOT</u> SIGN.
Why <u>don't</u> you <u>take</u> an ASL class? [negative question Aux]	-----------------------------WQ----------------------------- <u>WHY-NOT</u> YOU TAKE-UP ASL CLASS?

Additional English examples:

The 1880 Milan Conference ban<u>ned</u> signed languages in school, <u>didn't</u> it? [tag question]

Yes, it <u>did</u> (<u>no other</u> Aux, so "To Do" *is used as affirmative, same tense*).

English-ASL Note: "Did" *is an accepted auxiliary used for <u>emphasis</u> or <u>increased</u> <u>intensity</u>. In ASL it is <u>always</u> fingerspelled. The emphatic "do" is <u>not</u> used in present tense in ASL.*

English	ASL
Courtney <u>did</u> show up.	1) COURTNEY [fs] <u>DID</u> [fs] SHOW-UP. 2) COURTNEY [fs] <u>TRUE</u> SHOW-UP. 3) COURTNEY [fs] <u>TRUE-BUSINESS</u> SHOW-UP.
We <u>did</u> pass the final exam!	----------T---------- 1) FINAL EXAM, WE <u>DID</u> [fs] PASS! ----------T---------- 2) FINAL EXAM, WE <u>TRUE</u> PASS! ----------T---------- 3) FINAL EXAM, WE <u>TRUE-BUSINESS</u> PASS!
Leslie <u>does</u> want to go to summer school.	LESLIE [fs] <u>WANT</u> (signed with emphasis) GO SUMMER SCHOOL.
I <u>do</u> taste sugar in the tea.	1) YES, I TASTE SUGAR THERE TEA. 2) I <u>TRUE</u> TASTE SUGAR THERE TEA.

Auxiliary Verbs: Modals

English-ASL Notes: *1) The* **modal** *auxiliaries indicate the advisability, necessity, permissibility, possibility or probability of something. Their use constitutes a* **conditional tense.**

English Example: We <u>can</u>/<u>had better</u>/<u>have to</u>/<u>must</u>/<u>need to</u>/<u>ought to</u>/<u>should</u> pay taxes.

Note: [*] *indicates modal used in ASL as well.*

28

be able to	be going to	(be) *supposed (to)	*can/may
could	had better	have to/have got to	*maybe
*might	*must	*#OK	*should
*need to	ought to	*used to	would (rather)

2) In ASL, a modal *can* be placed either <u>before</u> the verb or <u>at the end of the sentence</u>, or both, for emphasis.

English	ASL
You <u>should/ought to</u> hire an interpreter.	1) YOU <u>SHOULD</u> HIRE INTERPRETER. 2) YOU HIRE INTERPRETER <u>SHOULD</u>. 3) YOU <u>SHOULD</u> HIRE INTERPRETER <u>SHOULD</u>.

Auxiliary Verb: "Used To"

English-ASL Note: The auxiliary "used to" expresses a past habit or condition that no longer exists. It is followed by the infinitive (base) form of the verb. ASL signs FORMER, PAST or PAST HABIT.

English	ASL
CSD Fremont <u>used to be</u> in Berkeley.	FREMONT DEAF-SCHOOL <u>PAST</u> THERE BERKELEY.
They <u>used to smoke</u> but they quit.	1) THEY <u>PAST HABIT</u> SMOKE BUT QUIT. 2) THEY <u>FORMER</u> SMOKE BUT QUIT.

VERB TENSES

Verb Tense: Simple Present [Pres t]

English Note: The present tense form of a <u>regular</u> English verb looks exactly like the infinitive.

English Exception: **Third person singular present tense *adds* /-s/.**

English Example: **"to jump" present tense:**

Person	Singular	Plural
1st (speaker)	I jump	we jump
2nd (listener)	you jump	you jump
3rd (topic)	he, she, it jump<u>s</u>	they jump

ASL Note: *ASL does not have the third person singular ending /-s/.*

English	ASL
Kelly hope<u>s</u> to go to CSD Riverside.	KELLY [fs] <u>HOPE</u> GO RIVERSIDE-DEAF-SCHOOL.
The dog need<u>s</u> to go for a walk.	1) DOG <u>NEED</u> WALK. 2) DOG <u>NEED GO</u> WALK.

Verb Tense: Simple Past [Past t]

English-ASL Note: **Simple past tense *is used for actions <u>begun and completed</u> in the past.***

English Note: **For <u>regular</u> verbs, *add the past suffix* [-ed] *to the infinitive for <u>all</u> persons.***

English Example: **"to jump" past tense:**

Person	Singular	Plural
1st	I jump<u>ed</u>	we jump<u>ed</u>
2nd	you jump<u>ed</u>	you jump<u>ed</u>
3rd	he, she, it jump<u>ed</u>	they jump<u>ed</u>

ASL Note: *ASL can use* present tense verbs *for both* <u>past</u> *and* <u>present</u> tenses.

English	ASL
I <u>wanted to know</u> if my boss <u>called</u>.	I <u>WANT KNOW</u> IF MY BOSS <u>FINISH</u> <u>TTY-ME</u>.
We <u>had a good</u> breakfast this morning.	NOW MORNING WE <u>HAVE</u> GOOD BREAKFAST.

ASL Exceptions—verb tenses that require a change in mouth movement:

BEAR/BORN	BREAK/BROKE	CATCH/CAUGHT
FIND/FOUND	FORGET/FORGOT	GET/GOT
GO, #GO/WENT/GONE	LEAVE/LEFT	LOSE/LOST
SEE/SAW	SELL/SOLD	SHOOT/SHOT
STEAL/STOLE	TAKE/TOOK	TEAR/TORE
TELL/TOLD	THINK/THOUGHT	WIN/WON

English	ASL
I <u>saw</u> you at deaf bowling.	I <u>SAW</u> YOU THERE DEAF BOWL++.
Frankie <u>was born</u> in Utah.	1) FRANKIE [fs] <u>BORN</u> UTAH. 2) FRANKIE [fs] <u>BORN</u> THERE UTAH.
Sandy <u>received</u> a hearing dog.	SANDY [fs] <u>GOT</u> HEARING DOG.

Verb Tense: Future [Fut t]

English-ASL Note: *Both English and ASL indicate future tense with "will."* *English puts this future auxiliary <u>in front of the verb</u>, but ASL can also put it <u>at the end</u>.*

English Notes: *1) The <u>first</u> auxiliary takes the tense. The verb itself then goes into the infinitive (base) form.*

English	ASL
Clare <u>will prepare</u> lunch for us.	1) CLARE [fs] <u>WILL COOK</u> LUNCH FOR US. 2) CLARE [fs] <u>COOK</u> LUNCH FOR US <u>WILL</u>.
The National Theatre of the Deaf <u>will hold</u> rehearsals for their new play.	1) NTD <u>WILL HAVE</u> REHEARSAL FOR NEW PLAY. 2) NTD <u>HAVE</u> REHEARSAL FOR NEW PLAY <u>WILL</u>.

2) English also uses the informal auxiliary "Be Going To" to express future tense. ASL does <u>not</u> have this expression.

English	ASL
We <u>are going to study</u> in the library.	WE <u>WILL</u> STUDY THERE LIBRARY.

<u>ASL Note:</u> *"**Will**" is not expressed if future tense is <u>understood</u>.*

English	ASL
Morgan <u>will take</u> interpreting classes next year.	---------TI--------- NEXT-YEAR, MORGAN [fs] <u>TAKE-UP</u> INTERPRETING CLASS.
Tomorrow morning we <u>will be going</u> to Sea World.	--------------------TI---------------------- TOMORROW MORNING, WE <u>GO</u> SEA WORLD.

<u>Verb Tenses: Perfect [Perf t]</u>: ("To Have" + /-ed, -en/)

<u>English Notes:</u> *1) In English, perfect tenses are variations of past tense, indicating actions begun in the past. (ASL has no perfect tenses; the tense expressed for present and past perfect is the simple past, p. 29.)*

2) There are four perfect tenses: <u>present</u> [Pres Perf t], <u>past</u> [Past Perf t], <u>future</u> [Fut Perf t] and <u>conditional</u> [Cond Perf t].

3) The first three are composed of the present, past or future of the auxiliary "To Have" + the infinitive (base) form of the verb + the past participle of the verb, /-ed, -en/. Conditional perfect tense is composed of a <u>modal auxiliary</u> + verb + /-ed, -en/.

4) Present perf tense expresses an *action begun in the past and finished in the present; the* auxiliary "To Have" *is in the present* tense.

ASL Note: **Perfect tenses** *are* **expressed** *by* **the** *simple past tense* **marker, FINISH.**

English	ASL
The students <u>have studied</u> for the ASL test. (Pres Perf t)	1) STUDENT <u>FINISH STUDY</u> FOR ASL TEST. 2) STUDENT <u>STUDY FINISH</u> FOR ASL TEST. 3) STUDENT <u>STUDY</u> FOR ASL TEST <u>FINISH</u>. 4) <u>FINISH</u> STUDENT <u>STUDY</u> FOR ASL TEST.

5) Past perfect tense expresses an action *begun in the past and finished before another past action* occurred; the auxiliary **"To Have"** *is in the past* tense.

English Example:

The ASL students <u>had studied</u> for the Deaf culture test for three nights. Their professor <u>had</u> already <u>taught</u> their class about principles of Deaf culture.

English	ASL
When we <u>arrived</u> at the theater, the movie <u>had</u> already <u>started.</u>	HAPPEN WE <u>ARRIVE</u> MOVIE HOUSE, MOVIE <u>FINISH START</u>.

6) Future perfect tense expresses an action *to be completed in the future before another action further in the future* occurs. **The future auxiliary "will"** *is used and* **"To Have"** *is in the* **infinitive,** *since only the* <u>first</u> **auxiliary verb** *in any verb phrase can be conjugated.* **The verb** *itself goes into the* **past participle /-ed, -en/ form.**

English Example:

By the time the students take the ASL test, they <u>will have studied</u> for six hours.

English	ASL
When we arrive tomorrow, we <u>will have driven</u> for two days.	HAPPEN TOMORROW WE ARRIVE, WE <u>FINISH DRIVE</u> TWO DAY.

7) <u>Conditional perfect tense</u> *expresses an action that was <u>possible, probable or advisable in the <u>past</u>; the* auxiliary *is a* modal, *"To Have" is in the* infinitive, *and the verb is in the* past participle */-ed, -en/ form.*

English Example:

The students <u>could not have</u> earn<u>ed</u> such high test scores without studying. (neg)

English	ASL
Looking back, I <u>should have</u> tak<u>en</u> more math.	LOOK-BACK, I SHOULD <u>FINISH TAKE-UP</u> MORE MATH.

Verb Tenses: Progressive/Continuous [Cont t] ("To Be" + /-ing/)

English-ASL Note: Progressive, *or* **continuous tenses [Cont t]** *indicate that an action either is repetitive or has been recurring for some time.*

English Notes: *I) The* continuous tense *is composed of the* auxiliary *"To Be" plus the* present participle *of the verb, /-ing/ suffix.*

2) *There are* **four** continuous tenses: <u>present</u> **[Pres Cont]**, <u>past</u> **[Past Cont]**, <u>future</u> **[Fut Cont]** *and* <u>conditional</u> **[Cond Cont].**

3) *For* present continuous, *"To Be" is in the* <u>present</u> *tense; for* past continuous, *it is in the* <u>past</u> *tense and the* verb *is in the* present participle */-ing/ form.*

ASL Note: *For a visual language, the* sign itself *is repeated* **[++].** *ASL has no auxiliary "To Be" and no /-ing/ participial ending.* <u>Head nodding</u> **[--Y--]** *may accompany. (See Inflected Verbs section, p. 24)*

English	ASL
The alarm clock light <u>is</u> flash<u>ing</u>. [Pres Cont t]	ALARM <u>FLASH</u>++.
All day yesterday Mother <u>was</u> cook<u>ing</u>. [Past Cont t]	------------------TI------------------ YESTERDAY ALL-DAY MOTHER ------y------ <u>COOK</u>++.

4) *For future continuous, the auxiliary "will" takes the tense, rendering "To Be" in the* infinitive, *because only the <u>first</u> auxiliary verb in any verb phrase can be conjugated.*

English Examples:

Sidney <u>will be</u> major<u>ing</u> in ASL/Deaf Studies at CSUN. [Fut Cont t]

The campus coffee house <u>will be</u> offer<u>ing</u> a 10% discount this Friday. [Fut Cont t]

> **5) The conditional modal _takes the tense, rendering "To Be" in the infinitive (base) form._**

English	ASL
Deaf actor Bernard Bragg <u>might be</u> perform<u>ing</u> in a new movie. [Cond Cont t]	DEAF ACTOR B-B <u>MAYBE</u> <u>PERFORM</u> NEW MOVIE.
Ricky <u>should be</u> think<u>ing</u>. [Cond Cont t]	----------------Y---------------- 1) RICKY [fs] <u>SHOULD THINK++</u>. --------------------Y-------------------- 2) RICKY [fs] <u>SHOULD THINK-ABOUT</u>.

PARTICIPLES [Part]

Gerunds: Present Participles Functioning as Nouns

English Note: **The /-ing/ form of the verb can be used as a noun in all the parts of a sentence where nouns function: subject [S], direct object of the verb [DO], predicate noun [PN], or object of the preposition [OP], but not as indirect object of the verb.**

ASL Notes: 1) **ASL Gerunds have no /-ing/ suffix.**

  2) **ASL Gerunds are generally signed with a <u>double</u> movement.**

English	ASL
Stop <u>eating</u>. [DO]	<u>EAT++</u> STOP.
<u>Swimming</u> is good exercise. [S]	<u>SWIM++</u> GOOD EXERCISE.
We like <u>singing</u>. [DO]	WE LIKE <u>SING++</u>.
Dana won a trophy for <u>running</u>. [OP]	DANA [fs] WON TROPHY FOR <u>RUN++</u>.

Madison finished <u>watching</u> the movie.	-----T----- MOVIE MADISON [fs] FINISH <u>WATCH</u>. (single movement)

Present and Past Participles Functioning as Adjectives

English Note: Both the present participle /-ing/ and the past participle /-ed, -en/ forms of the verb can function as adjectives [Adj], either modifying a noun or as a predicate adjective [PA].

ASL Note: ASL does not have either /-ing/ or /-ed, -en/ participial endings.

English	ASL
1) The class is bor<u>ing</u>/excit<u>ing</u>/confus<u>ing</u>. [PA] 2) The bor<u>ing</u>/excit<u>ing</u>/confus<u>ing</u> class (Adj)	CLASS <u>BORE/EXCITE/CONFUSE</u>.
1) The students are bor<u>ed</u>/excit<u>ed</u>/ confus<u>ed</u>. [PA] 2) The bor<u>ed</u>/excit<u>ed</u>/confus<u>ed</u> students (Adj)	STUDENT THEY <u>BORE/EXCITE/ CONFUSE</u>.

Verbs: Contractions

English-ASL Note: English can have either <u>full verb</u> spelling or <u>contracted</u> verbs, such as: I have ~ I've, I will ~ I'll, I should not ~ I shouldn't, etc. This is <u>not</u> true for ASL.

English	ASL
1) We <u>cannot/can't</u> do that.	-----N----- 1) WE <u>CAN'T</u> DO THAT.
2) We <u>should not/shouldn't</u> do that.	-----------N------------ 2) WE <u>SHOULD NOT</u> DO THAT.
I<u>'ve</u> been there.	1) I <u>FINISH</u> TOUCH. 2) I TOUCH <u>FINISH</u>.
They<u>'ll</u> check the mail.	THEY <u>WILL</u> CHECK MAIL.
She<u>'d</u> want to go shopping.	SHE <u>WANT</u> GO SHOP++.

ASL Exceptions: **CAN'T** and **WON'T**

```
------T-----              ---------N---------
```
SHRIMP, I ALLERGIC, <u>CAN'T EAT.</u>

```
      ----------------N----------------
```
WE <u>WILL NOT/WON'T</u> BUY THAT-ONE.

Verbs: Directional

ASL Notes: *1) Only certain verb signs can be moved in any direction:*

ASK	BLAME	BORROW/LEND	BRING
CALL/PHONE	CALL/SUMMON	COMPARE	COPY
DRIVE	GIVE	HIRE/INVITE/WELCOME	
HELP	LOOK	MEET	MOVE
PAY	SEND/SEND	SHOW	TAKE-ADVANTAGE
TEACH	TELL	THROW	VISIT

English	ASL
I'll <u>meet</u> you at the Deaf club.	<u>I-MEET-YOU</u> THERE DEAF #CLUB.
When I sign, you should <u>look at</u> my face.	----------CC---------- WHEN I SIGN, <u>YOU-LOOK-ME</u> MY FACE SHOULD.

*2) **Partial-directional** verb signs have limited movement options in direction:*

COME	DISCUSS	GO	READ

3) Non-directional verbs *include:*

COMPLAIN	EAT	FEEL	GET	HAVE
LIVE	NEED	PLAY	SAY	WANT

English	ASL
Deaf people <u>live</u> in peace next to the noisy street.	------------------------T------------------- DEAF CLOSE NOISY STREET <u>LIVE</u> PEACE.
More and more interpreters <u>are needed</u> nationwide. [Pres t Passive]	-----y----- WE <u>NEED</u> MORE++ INTERPRETER NATION ALL-OVER.

Noun-Verb Pairs with a Change in Movement

<u>ASL Note</u>: **A noun [N]** *sign requires* <u>multiple</u> *movements. A verb* **[V]** *sign requires* <u>one</u> *movement. Below is a partial list of ASL examples.*

Nouns	Verbs/Adjectives/Adverbs
ADDRESS/RESIDENCE	LIVE/RESIDE
ADVICE	ADVISE
ASSISTANCE	ASSIST
DRILL	DRILL
EQUALITY	EQUAL
HEATER/HEATING	HEAT
KEY/LOCK	LOCK
MEASUREMENT/SIZE	MEASURE
OVEN	BAKE
PLANT	GROW
PRAYER	PRAY

SPEED	FAST
STAPLER	STAPLE
STORY	TELL-STORY
TASTE	TASTE

ASL Examples:

CAN YOU <u>ADVISE</u> US? (1x for V)
CAN <u>YOU-ADVISE-ME</u> US? (1x for V)
WE NEED GOOD <u>ADVICE</u>. (2x for N)

I NOW <u>BAKE</u> COOKIE. (1x for V)
PLEASE <u>OVEN</u> TURN-ON. (2x for N)

YOU SIGN <u>FAST.</u> (1x for Adv)
<u>SPEED</u> FOR YOUR SIGN SLOW. (several x for N)

<u>HELP</u> YOURSELF. (1x for V)
I NEED YOUR <u>HELP</u>. (several x for N)

TEA <u>TASTE</u> GOOD. (1x for V)
YOU HAVE GOOD <u>TASTE</u> FOR CLOTHES. (2x for N)

SIXTY MINUTE <u>EQUAL</u> ONE HOUR. (1x for V)
PEOPLE LIKE <u>EQUALITY</u>. (several x for N)

<u>SIZE</u> WHAT? (2x for N)
I DON'T-KNOW; <u>MEASURE</u> MUST. (1x for V)

I NEED <u>PRAYER</u>. (2x for N)
PLEASE <u>PRAY</u> FOR ME. (1x for V)

THIS ROOM <u>HOT.</u> (1x for Adj)
PLEASE, <u>HEATER</u> TURN-OFF. (2x for N)
HIS NEW JOB <u>HEATING</u>, AC. (2x for N)

LB (LONG BEACH), MY FRIEND <u>LIVE/RESIDE</u>. (1x for V)
LB <u>ADDRESS/RESIDENCE</u> WHAT? (2x for N)

YOU HAVE <u>STAPLER</u>? (2x for N)
THESE CARD <u>STAPLE</u> PLEASE. (1x for V)

MY DENTIST USE NEW <u>DRILL</u>. (2x for N)
HE <u>DRILL</u> MY TEETH TWO. (1x for V)

WE BUY FIVE <u>PLANT</u>. (2x for N)
WE <u>GROW</u> FLOWER ALL-OVER. (1x for V)

JERRELL [fs] LOSE <u>KEY</u>. (2x for N)
HE NEED <u>LOCK</u> OFFICE. (1x for V)

CHILDREN KISS-FIST GOOD <u>STORY</u>. (2x for N)
THEMSELVES OFTEN <u>TELL-STORY</u>. (2x for V)

ASL Exceptions:

<u>CLEAN/CLEAN-UP</u> (several x for V)
<u>CLEAN</u> (1x for Adj)

<u>PAGE</u> (ix or 2x short for N)
<u>LOOK-UP</u> (2x or more long for V)

<u>CALM</u> (1x for Adj)
<u>CALM-DOWN</u> (2x for V)

Noun-Verb Pairs with No Change in Movement

ASL Examples:

Nouns	Verbs
BELIEF	BELIEVE
COMPLAINT	COMPLAIN
DANCE	DANCE
DISAPPEARANCE	DISAPPEAR
ENTERTAINMENT/ENJOYMENT	ENTERTAIN/ENJOY
INCREASE	INCREASE
INTEREST/FASCINATION	INTEREST/FASCINATE
INTRODUCTION	INTRODUCE

ORDER	ORDER
PENCIL SHARPENER	SHARPEN-PENCIL
PERMISSION	PERMIT
RAIN	RAIN
SIGHT/VISION	SEE
SONG, MUSIC	SING
STUDIES	STUDY
SUGGESTION	SUGGEST
THEFT	STEAL
WORK	WORK

Verbs: Active ~ Passive Voice

English Notes: 1) **Active** *voice* *means that the* **subject [S], or agent,** *is performing the action, or transitive verb* **[Vt],** *upon the* **receiver, or Direct Object of the Verb [DO]: The dog bit the man [S Vt DO].**

2) **Passive** *voice* *is used: for general statements or announcements, like this one; when the agent/actor is unknown, obvious or unimportant; or when the* **direct object** *is being emphasized.*

3) **Passive** *voice* *is formed by putting the* **direct object** *into* **subject [S]** *position and changing the* **active verb** *to the* **corresponding tense [t] of "To Be" [Vbe],** *plus the* **past participle /-ed, -en/: The man was bitten (by the dog).**

4) The **agent** *may either be deleted or appear as the object of the preposition "by" in an* **adverbial prepositional phrase** *at the end, like the example in 3) above.*

English Examples:

Active Voice	Passive Voice
The ASL Department is offering night classes. [Pres Cont t]	Night classes are being offered by the ASL Department. (general statement) [Pres Cont Passive t]

Someone <u>stole</u> my car last night. [Past t]	My car <u>was stolen</u> last night. (agent unknown) [Past Passive t]
The police <u>have caught</u> the thief. [Pres Perf t]	The thief <u>has been caught</u>. (agent obvious) [Pres Perf Passive t]
Two ASL instructors <u>wrote</u> this book. [Past t]	This book <u>was written</u> by two ASL instructors. (DO being emphasized) [Past Passive t]

<u>ASL Note</u>: *There is no specific* **passive voice structure** *in ASL; all sentences are in* **active voice,** *meaning the actor remains in* **subject position.**

English	ASL
My house <u>was listed</u> by a realtor.	REALTOR <u>LIST</u> MY HOUSE <u>FINISH</u>.
I <u>was told</u> by someone else.	OTHER PERSON <u>TOLD</u> ME.
Bill <u>is survived by</u> his wife, Tammy.	BILL [fs] <u>DIE</u>, BUT HIS WIFE, TAMMY [fs], STILL <u>LIVE</u>.
Light refreshments <u>will be served</u>.	<u>WILL SERVE</u> SMALL FOOD. (actor irrelevant)

<u>ASL Exceptions</u>: *1)* **MAKE/BUILD BY** *and* **WRITE BY;** **"BY"** *is fingerspelled:*

GARAGE <u>BUILD</u> <u>BY</u> [fs] FATHER.

BOOK <u>WRITE</u> <u>BY</u> [fs] MEL [fs].

2) **Passive voice** *can be expressed through* **directional verbs.**

English	ASL
This animal <u>is called</u> a barn owl.	THIS ANIMAL <u>CALL</u> BARN [fs] OWL.
I <u>was given</u> many gifts.	MANY GIFT <u>GIVE-ME</u>++.

ADVERBS [Adv]

<u>Note</u>: **Adverbs** *can be either single words, phrases or clauses. Their function is to* **modify verbs.**

Adverbs: Manner

English-ASL Notes: 1) <u>Adverbs of manner</u> *describe* <u>how</u> *the action is performed.* *(See Inflected Verbs section, p. 24.)*

English	ASL
You fingerspell <u>fast</u>.	YOU FINGERSPELL <u>FAST</u>.
Please read slow<u>ly</u>.	1) PLEASE READ <u>SLOW</u>. 2) PLEASE <u>READ-SLOW</u>. ("read" signed slowly with intense facial expression)
She told me repeated<u>ly</u>.	SHE-<u>TELL-ME++</u>. (signed with effort)
My brother eats <u>non-stop</u>.	MY BROTHER <u>EAT-CONTINUOUS</u>. (circled)
My brother eats <u>all the time</u>.	MY BROTHER <u>EAT-REPEAT.</u> (stop-and-go action)

2) *English adverbs of manner often end in the marker* **[-ly]. ASL adverbs do** <u>not</u> **have this marker. They can be expressed with mouth morphemes, however. (See pp. 114 ff.)**

English	ASL
Adrian draws beautiful<u>ly</u>.	ADRIAN [fs] DRAW <u>BEAUTIFUL</u>.
They came here recent<u>ly</u>.	1) <u>RECENT</u> THEY COME-HERE. 2) THEY COME-HERE <u>RECENT</u>.
Normal<u>ly</u>/natural<u>ly</u>	<u>NORMAL/NATURAL</u>

Adverbs: Comparatives/Superlatives

English-ASL Notes: 1) *The comparative and superlative forms of adverbs [Adv] are used to compare two or more verbs.*

2) *For the* <u>equivalent</u> *comparison of an adverb, use* **[as (Adv)** <u>as</u> **(N)]. ASL can also use SAME.**

3) *For the English comparative form of an adverb, add* **[-er than]** *to the adverb.*

4) For the English superlative form of an adverb, add [the (Adv) -est] (of all). Note: "of all" is optional and is used in ASL to indicate emphasis.

<u>*English Examples:*</u>

Donnie types <u>as</u> fast <u>as</u> Addison but <u>more slowly than</u> Dale; Whitney types <u>the</u> fast<u>est of all</u>.

<u>*ASL Notes:*</u> *1) ASL does not have the English adverb marker [-ly].*

2) ASL does not use "the" in the superlative form.

English	ASL
My teacher fingerspells <u>as</u> clearly <u>as</u> yours.	1) MY TEACHER FINGERSPELL CLEAR <u>AS-AS/SAME</u> YOURS. 2) MY TEACHER [ix-L], YOURS [ix-R] FINGERSPELL <u>SAME-LEFT-RIGHT</u>.
Dane fingerspells <u>more</u> clear<u>ly than</u> Jo.	1) DANE [fs] FINGERSPELL <u>MORE</u> CLEAR <u>THAN</u> JO [fs]. 2) DANE [fs] [ix-L], JO [fs] [ix-R], POINT-L FINGERSPELL <u>MORE</u> CLEAR.
Marian fingerspells <u>the most</u> clear<u>ly</u>.	1) MARIAN [fs] SHE FINGERSPELL <u>MOST</u> CLEAR. 2) MARIAN [fs] SHE FINGERSPELL CLEAR<u>EST</u>.
I fingerspell the fast<u>est</u> but <u>the worst</u>.	I FINGERSPELL FAST<u>EST</u> BUT <u>WORST</u>. (scrunched facial expression at end)

Adverbs: Intensifiers

<u>*English-ASL Note:*</u> **Intensifiers are adverbs [Adv] *that modify other* adverbs or adjectives [Adj]. They <u>precede</u> the word they modify, forming adverb phrases or adjective phrases. [*] indicates that ASL shares these intensifiers.**

absolutely	*(a) little (bit)	*extremely	fairly	*less
*more	*most	pretty	quite	rather
*really	somewhat/*so-so	*too	unbelievably	very

English	ASL
I accept your apology, but <u>somewhat</u> skeptical<u>ly</u>. (Adv, Adv)	YOUR APOLOGY I ACCEPT, BUT <u>LITTLE-BIT</u> SKEPTIC.

ASL Note: 1) The glossed hyphen is an indication of "very," which does not really belong in ASL. When "very" is implied, the <u>adjective sign</u> needs to gain in strength and speed, and the <u>facial expression</u> needs to intensify. Also there is a head movement beginning at the dominant side when the sign starts and ending forward when the sign releases.

English	ASL
I was <u>very</u> sick last week.	---------TI--------- LAST-WEEK I <u>VERY-SICK</u>.

2) *Sign* WOW, REAL/REALLY, WORSE *or* TOO MUCH/EXTREME.

English	ASL
Death Valley is <u>really</u> hot in the summer.	DURING SUMMER, DEATH VALLEY <u>WOW</u> HOT.
My father works <u>harder</u> than my uncle.	1) MY FATHER WORK <u>WORSE</u> THAN MY UNCLE. 2) MY FATHER <u>WORK++</u>, MY UNCLE SO-SO.
ASL has <u>extremely complicated</u> grammar.	ASL HAVE GRAMMAR <u>EXTREME COMPLICATE</u>.

3) *Fingerspell* TOO; *intensify facial expression.*

English	ASL
The pie is <u>too</u> sweet for me.	1) PIE <u>TOO</u> [fs] SWEET FOR ME. 2) PIE <u>SWEET</u> (grimace) FOR ME.
It's <u>too</u> cold outside.	OUTSIDE <u>COLD</u>. (grimace)

Adverbs: Negation

<u>ASL Notes</u>: 1) The negative signs for "not" can be left out while preserving the negative non-verbal behaviors.

2) Use **NOT** *to replace negative prefixes (dis-, il-, in-, im-, ir-, un-, etc.).* *(See section on* **Prefixes** *on p.79.)*

3) Use **CAN'T** *for "cannot."*

4) **WON'T** *and* **REFUSE** *share with same sign with each word mouthed appropriately.* **WON'T** *adds negative non-verbal behavior.* **REFUSE** *adds scrunched eyebrows and pursed lips without negative headshake.*

5) *A few signs attach a "throw-away" affix to become negative:*

DON'T-LIKE	DON'T-KNOW	DON'T-WANT
ILLEGAL	WITHOUT	WORTHLESS

6) *These signs use the 2-hand* **NONE** *instead of the throw-away affix:*

English	ASL
faithless	FAITH NONE
faultless	FAULT NONE
fearless	FEAR NONE
guiltless	GUILT NONE
homeless	HOME NONE
hopeless	HOPE NONE
limitless	LIMIT NONE
loveless	LOVE NONE
merciless	MERCY NONE
selfless	SELFISH NONE
sinless	SIN NONE

7) *The following are some negative options:*

PAY MONEY A-LOT, I CAN'T.
                DON'T.
                DON'T-LIKE.
                DON'T-WANT.
                NEVER.
                #NO; SAY-NO (forward).
                NONE.
                NOT.
                NOTHING.
                NOT-YET.
                REFUSE.
                WON'T.

Adverbs: Frequency

ALWAYS	EVERY-DAY/WEEK/MONTH/YEAR	
EVERY-MORNING/AFTERNOON/NIGHT		OFTEN
EVERY-(2)-DAYS	RARELY	SOMETIMES

English-ASL Note: Adverbs of frequency can occur at either the <u>beginning</u> or the <u>end</u> of a sentence.

English	ASL
1) I go to work <u>every morning</u>.	1) I GO WORK <u>EVERY-MORNING</u>.
2) <u>Every morning</u> I go to work.	2) <u>EVERY-MORNING</u> I GO WORK.
Lonnie attends the NAD conference <u>every other year</u>.	LONNIE [fs] ATTEND NAD CONFERENCE <u>EVERY-TWO-YEAR</u>.
<u>Every fall</u> we bake pumpkin pies.	<u>EVERY-YEAR</u> FALL WE BAKE PUMPKIN PIE.
Night<u>ly</u>; week<u>ly</u>; month<u>ly</u>	<u>EVERY-NIGHT</u>; <u>EVERY-WEEK</u>; <u>EVERY-MONTH</u>

Adverbs: Clock Time

ASL Notes: 1) Flip 10, 11 and 12 <u>once</u> for 10:05, 11:05, 12:05. Flip <u>once or twice</u> for 10:00, 11:00, 12:00.

2) For "a.m." sign MORNING; for "p.m." sign AFTERNOON or NIGHT, _as appropriate_.

English	ASL
The local news is broadcast <u>at 6:00 p.m.</u>	1) LOCAL NEWS ANNOUNCE <u>TIME 6 NIGHT</u>. 2) LOCAL NEWS ANNOUNCE <u>TIME-6 NIGHT</u>.
	----------------------TI--------------------------
The fingerspelling class meets today <u>at 11:00 a.m.</u>	<u>TODAY, TIME 11:00 MORNING</u>, FINGERSPELLING CLASS MEET.

Adverbs: Early, Mid-, Late

English	ASL
Early in the day	MORNING
Late in the day	AFTERNOON/EVENING
Late Friday	FRIDAY NIGHT
Early in the week	SUNDAY – TUESDAY
Late in the month	LAST ONE-WEEK MONTH
Late 1990s	1997-1999, 97-99
Early 2015	WINTER 2015, 15
Mid-year	SUMMER
Late 2020	FALL 2020, 20

Introductory Adverbial Time/Tense Indicators

ASL Notes: _1) In general,_ place time indicators _at the_ _beginning_ _of the sentence, to set up the tense,_ _and_ _raise eyebrows. Once a timeframe has been established, it is assumed to continue through all the following sentences until a new time is set up._

2) If there is no time indicator in the sentence, the _present_ _tense is assumed._

3) This rule applies to past, present _and_ future _tenses,_ _but not to vague time concepts, such as_ anytime, later, long ago, soon, recently, etc., _or to frequency time concepts, such as_ every day, monthly, biweekly, etc.

4) Begin with the _broadest_ _category of time and move to the_ _narrowest_:
LAST WEEK, FRIDAY, TIME-7:00 MORNING.
5) Symbol --- TI --- [with _raised_ _eyebrows]_

English	ASL
We visited Deaf West Theatre <u>yesterday</u>.	---------TI--------- <u>YESTERDAY</u>, WE VISIT DWT.

48

| | ---------TI-------- |
| Gallaudet University opened in 1864. | BACK 1864, GALLAUDET OPEN. |

| | ----------TI---------- |
| We will leave for summer school tomorrow. | TOMORROW WE LEAVE FOR SUMMER SCHOOL. |

ASL Exceptions: *The time indicator can be placed at the end for short sentences or questions. Do not raise eyebrows.*

English	ASL
We must study for a test next week. (indicating time of test, not of study)	1) WE MUST STUDY FOR TEST NEXT-WEEK. 2) HAVE TEST NEXT-WEEK; WE MUST STUDY.
See you later/tomorrow.	SEE YOU LATER/TOMORROW. (very brief sentence)
Did your daughter graduate yesterday?	---------------------------Q------------------------ YOUR DAUGHTER GRADUATE --------------------- YESTERDAY?
Jordan worked for three hours. [Adv Prep Phr]	JORDAN [fs] work THREE-HOUR FINISH.

ASL Note: *Replace English time indicators "in" or "on" with* **PAST/BACK** *or* **FUTURE.**

English	ASL
In 1966	PAST/BACK 1966
In 2019	FUTURE 2019
In the morning	THIS/TOMORROW MORNING, DURING MORNING
This past week	LAST-WEEK
On/for Thursday	THURSDAY, LAST THURSDAY, THIS THURSDAY/THIS-WEEK THURSDAY, NEXT THURSDAY/NEXT-WEEK THURSDAY

<u>On</u>/<u>for</u> March 1st	MARCH 1ST, <u>FOR</u> MARCH 1ST, <u>LAST</u> MARCH 1ST
<u>This</u> March 1st	<u>NEXT</u> MARCH 1ST/<u>NEXT-YEAR</u> MARCH 1ST

ASL Note: The preposition sign **ON** *indicates a surface or "on top of," so it does* <u>not</u> *function as an adverb of time. Similarly, the preposition sign* **IN** *indicates "inside of," so it does* <u>not</u> *function as an adverb of time, either.*

English	ASL
I have an appointment <u>on</u> Monday.	1) I HAVE APPOINTMENT <u>FOR/NEXT-WEEK/FUTURE</u> MONDAY. 2) I HAVE APPOINTMENT MONDAY.
We will see one another <u>in</u> a month.	1) WE SEE EACH-OTHER <u>NEXT-MONTH</u>. 2) WE SEE EACH-OTHER <u>ONE-MONTH FUTURE</u>.

CONJUNCTIONS [Conj]

Note: **Conjunctions** *are generally single words. Their function is to join similar grammatical structures.*

<u>Coordinating Conjunctions</u>

English Note: The coordinating conjunctions [Coord Conj]—"and," "but," "or" and "nor"—connect similar grammatical structures: nouns with nouns [N + N], verbs with verbs [V + V], etc., phrases with phrases [Phr + Phr], and clauses with clauses [Cl + Cl]. This is called <u>parallel structure</u>.

English Example:

Interpreting students <u>and</u> teachers [N + N] must sign <u>or</u> voice [V + V], as required, during class time <u>but</u> not during the break [Adv Prep Phr + Adv Prep Phr].

ASL Notes: 1) **AND** *is used sparingly in ASL, usually with nouns or adjectives, not verbs.*

2) **AND** *is also used for emphasis:* **I FINISH COOK YOUR FAVORITE DINNER <u>AND</u> I MAKE YOUR FAVORITE DESSERT.**

3) There are several substitutes for AND:

English	ASL
My brother likes red <u>and</u> white. [Adj, Adj]	1) MY BROTHER LIKE RED <u>AND</u> WHITE. 2) MY BROTHER LIKE RED <u>PLUS</u> WHITE. 3) MY BROTHER LIKE RED <u>ALSO</u> WHITE. 4) MY BROTHER LIKE RED-L, WHITE-R. (<u>shifting shoulders</u>) 5) MY BROTHER LIKE (<u>1</u>) RED, (<u>2</u>) WHITE. (ix fingers) 6) MY BROTHER LIKE <u>BOTH</u> RED, WHITE.

4) AND works with only <u>two</u> nouns or adjectives, <u>not</u> with three or more.

<u>ASL Examples:</u>

Grammatical ASL	Ungrammatical ASL
1) I LIKE TACO <u>AND</u> BURRITO. 2) I LIKE TACO, BURRITO, RICE [fs]. 3) I LIKE (<u>1</u>) TACO, (<u>2</u>) BURRITO, (<u>3</u>) RICE [fs]. (ix fingers)	I LIKE TACO, BURRITO <u>AND</u> RICE [fs].

5) Sometimes AND is deleted altogether, as illustrated above and below:

English	ASL
Black <u>and</u> white TV	BLACK WHITE TV
Half <u>and</u> half	HALF, HALF (move dominant)
M <u>&</u> Ms	M, M (move dominant)
Over <u>and</u> over again	AGAIN++
Short <u>and</u> sweet	SHORT, SWEET (1x, 1x)
Two <u>and</u> one-half	2 ½
More and more	MORE, MORE

6) **BUT** *functions the same in ASL as in English, indicating contrast.*

English	ASL
My clothes are formal <u>but</u> comfortable.	MY CLOTHES FORMAL <u>BUT</u> COMFORTABLE.
Clare loves signing <u>but</u> not interpreting.	CLARE [fs] KISS-FIST SIGN <u>BUT</u> NOT INTERPRET.

7) **For the coordinating conjunction "or,"** *ASL uses the* **loan sign #OR,** <u>ranking</u> *options or* **WHICH?** *ASL does* <u>not</u> *have "nor"; instead use* **NOT.**

English	ASL
Does your dog like beef <u>or</u> chicken flavored snacks?	1) YOUR DOG LIKE FOOD BEEF, CHICKEN, <u>WHICH</u>? 2) YOUR DOG LIKE FOOD WHICH: (<u>1</u>) BEEF, (<u>2</u>) CHICKEN? (ix fingers)
1) My dog likes <u>neither</u> beef <u>nor</u> chicken.	MY DOG <u>DOESN'T-LIKE</u> BEEF, <u>DOESN'T-LIKE</u> CHICKEN.
2) My dog likes <u>neither one</u>.	MY DOG <u>DISLIKE BOTH</u>.

Correlative Conjunctions

<u>*English Notes:*</u> *1)* **Correlative conjunctions** *occur in pairs:* **"both . . . and . . . ,"** **"not only . . . but also . . . ,"** **"either . . . or . . . ,"** **"neither . . . nor . . . ."**

2) **To maintain parallelism, the grammatical structure** <u>*following*</u> *the first item of the pair and the one* <u>*following*</u> *the second must be the* <u>*same*</u>: nouns, verbs, adjectives, adverbs, etc.

Correlative Conjunctions: "Both . . . and . . ."

<u>*ASL Note:*</u> *ASL signs* **BOTH** *but* <u>not</u> *"and."* **PLUS** *can also be used.*

English	ASL
<u>Both</u> deaf <u>and</u> hard of hearing students attend residential schools for the deaf. [Adj, Adj]	1) DEAF, HH <u>BOTH</u> GO DEAF-SCHOOL. 2) DEAF <u>PLUS</u> HH GO DEAF-SCHOOL.
ASL interpreters both <u>sign</u> and <u>voice</u>. [V, V]	1) ASL INTERPRETER SIGN, VOICE <u>BOTH</u>. 2) ASL INTERPRETER SIGN <u>PLUS</u> VOICE.

Correlative Conjunctions: "Not only . . . but also . . ."

ASL Note: ASL uses PLUS.

English	ASL
We sell <u>not only</u> coffee <u>but also</u> sandwiches and ice cream. [N, N]	WE SELL COFFEE <u>PLUS</u> SANDWICH, ICE-CREAM.
Deaf club activities include <u>not only</u> cards <u>but also</u> bowling and bingo. [N, N]	DEAF CLUB ACTIVITY INCLUDE CARD <u>PLUS</u> BOWL, BINGO [fs].

Correlative Conjunctions: "Either . . . or . . ."

ASL Note: ASL can use the sign EITHER, the loan sign #OR and ranking options.

English	ASL
The cat must <u>either</u> come in now <u>or</u> stay out all night. [V, V]	1) CAT MUST COME NOW, STAY-OUT ALL-NIGHT, <u>EITHER</u>. 2) CAT COME NOW <u>#OR</u> STAY-OUT ALL-NIGHT MUST. 3) CAT MUST (<u>1</u>) COME NOW, (<u>2</u>) STAY-OUT ALL-NIGHT. (ix fingers)

Correlative Conjunctions: "Neither . . . nor . . ."

ASL Note: ASL signs NOT for both "neither" and "nor" and adds negative non-verbal behavior.

English	ASL
The plane landed <u>neither</u> safely <u>nor</u> on time. [Adv, Adv Prep Phr]	----------------N----------------- 1) PLANE LAND SAFE, ON-TIME. --------------N-------------- ----------N---- 2) PLANE <u>NOT</u> LAND SAFE, <u>NOT</u> ON---------- TIME.
<u>Neither</u> you <u>nor</u> I can go.	----N---- YOU, I <u>CAN'T</u> GO.

Prepositions [Prep]

<u>Note</u>: **Prepositions *are* single words *or* phrases. *They* function *as relationship* words. *A* preposition *describes the relationship* between the noun or pronoun *following it, which is its* object, *and the rest of the sentence. The* preposition *and its* object *make up a* prepositional phrase [Prep Phr]. Prepositions and prepositional phrases *function only as* adjectives [Adj] *and* adverbs [Adv].**

<u>English Examples</u>:

The cat <u>on the sofa</u> is a Siamese. [Prep Phr functioning as Adj describing "cat"]

The cat is sitting <u>on the sofa</u>. [Prep Phr functioning as Adv telling where]

<u>ASL Notes</u>: *1) As a <u>general</u> rule for ASL, keep prepositions only for location.*

English	ASL
90% <u>of</u> the time; most <u>of</u> the time	90% TIME; MOST TIME
Class <u>of</u> 2017	CLASS 2017
Coldest place <u>in</u> the world	COLDEST PLACE WORLD
Grandfather died <u>of</u> lung cancer.	GRANDFATHER DIE <u>FROM</u> LUNG CANCER.
Giraffes eat leaves <u>off</u> trees.	GIRAFFE EAT LEAF <u>FROM</u> TREE.
I am not afraid <u>of</u> the snake.	I NOT AFRAID SNAKE.
Rickie's home is <u>in</u> Fremont.	RICKIE [FS] HOME <u>THERE</u> FREMONT.

Mary Jones of Los Angeles.	MARY JONES [fs] <u>FROM/LIVE</u> LA.
NTID is in Rochester.	NTID <u>THERE</u> ROCHESTER.
Mother-in-law	MOTHER LAW
I am proud of you.	I PROUD YOU.
It's not my cup of tea	NOT MY CUP TEA.
<u>On/for</u> Thursday	<u>NEXT/THIS/LAST</u> THURSDAY
<u>On/for</u> September 10	<u>NEXT/THIS/LAST</u> SEPT 10
One in ten	ONE <u>FOR</u> EVERY 10; 10%; 1/10
Corey, 26, died of cancer.	COREY [fs] OLD 26, DIE <u>FROM</u> CANCER.
Peace of mind	PEACE MIND/MIND PEACE
See you on Monday.	SEE YOU MONDAY.
She gave birth to a son.	SHE BIRTH/BORN SON.
Take care of yourself.	TAKE-CARE YOURSELF.
The pain is in my mouth.	PAIN-MOUTH. (PAIN signed at mouth)
They go home on Fridays.	1) <u>EVERY-FRIDAY</u> THEY GO HOME. 2) THEY GO HOME <u>EVERY-FRIDAY</u>.
It's none of your business.	NONE YOUR BUSINESS.

2) Prepositions *are often embedded in* classifiers.

English	ASL
The book is <u>under</u> the table.	TABLE CL:B, BOOK <u>CL:B-UNDER</u>.
A bird is sitting <u>on</u> the hood.	CAR CL:3, BIRD <u>CL:V-SIT</u>.

3) Replace "in" and "at" with a pointing index finger for specifying a place without a roof or other cover.

English	ASL
We saw our aunt in Riverside.	WE SAW OUR AUNT THERE (ix R) RIVERSIDE.
Meet you at the park.	I-MEET-YOU THERE (ix L) PARK [fs].

INTERJECTIONS

English-ASL Note: Interjections are exclamations of strong emotions that are single words or phrases, but not full sentences. (See Declarative Sentences: Exclamatory on p. 62.) They include expletives of all types: surprise, shock, anger, cursing, etc. They are signed faster and with stronger facial expression and body intensity.

English	ASL
Awesome!	AWESOME!
Good!	GOOD!
No way!	Waggle 5 hand/1 finger
Oh my gosh!	JAW-DROP!; SLAP CHEEK!
Stop it!	FINISH! (one hand)
What!	#WHAT!
Wow!	WOW!/#WOW!

SECTION TWO:
SYNTAX (PHRASE and CLAUSE STRUCTURES)

PHRASES [Phr]

**English Notes**: 1) A phrase is a group of words that function together as a unit but are **not** one of the six basic sentence patterns. They do **not** contain both a subject and a predicate.

2) There are noun phrases, adjective phrases, verb phrases, adverb phrases, infinitive phrases, and prepositional phrases. Each is considered below.

Noun Phrases [N Phr]

**English Notes**: 1) **Noun phrases** take either of two forms: article noun [Art **N**] or article adjective noun [Art Adj **N**].

**English Examples**:

(1) a class [Art N]; (2) an ASL class [Art Adj N]

(1) the boy [Art N]; (2) the deaf boy [Art Adj N]; (3) the tall deaf boy [Art Adj Adj N]

2) **Noun phrases** function as subject [**S**], direct object of the verb [**DO**], object of the preposition [**OP**] and predicate noun [**PN**].]

**ASL Note**: In ASL, noun phrases do **not** use articles. Definite articles are indicated by pointing/indexing [ix].

English	ASL
The boy is taking an ASL class. [S, DO]	BOY [ix L] TAKE-UP ASL CLASS.
The tall deaf boy is taking a class. [S, DO]	TALL DEAF BOY [ix L] TAKE-UP CLASS.
Jason is the tall deaf boy. [PN]	JASON [fs] [ix L] TALL DEAF BOY.

Verb Phrases [V Phr]

English Note: A verb phrase is two or more verbs working together as a unit. Generally this is comprised of the main verb plus its auxiliaries, any participial endings (/-ed, -en/; /-ing/), and any negative adverbs. It can also be two or more verbs joined together with a conjunction.

English Examples:

She <u>should not have been wasting</u> time. [S Vt DO, Cond Perf Cont t neg]

Certified Deaf Interpreters <u>sign</u> but <u>do not voice</u>. [Pres t, Conj, Pres t neg]

ASL Note: ASL has no participial endings, but does have auxiliaries to make verb phrases, including FINISH, PAST/BEFORE, WILL and modals.

English	ASL
We <u>will be going</u> to a silent weekend. [Fut Cont t]	WE <u>WILL GO</u> SILENT WEEKEND. [Fut t]
My old TV <u>did not have</u> captioning. [Past t neg]	---N--- MY OLD TV <u>BEFORE NOT HAVE</u> CC. [Past t neg]
You <u>ought to be taking</u> Deaf Culture. [Cond Cont t]	YOU <u>TAKE-UP</u> DEAF CULTURE CLASS <u>SHOULD</u>. [Cond t]

Infinitive Phrases [Inf Phr]

English Note: The infinitive, or "To" form of the verb, is already a phrase if the marker is present. Infinitive phrases function as nouns: subject [S], direct object of the verb [DO] and predicate noun [PN], but not as object of the preposition [OP]

ASL Notes: 1) ASL does not have the infinitive marker "To."

2) The infinitive is signed with a single movement; most verbs move once (1x), but some move 2x: COOK, DRIVE, PLAY, SWIM, etc.

English	ASL
Chris likes <u>to golf</u>. [<u>DO</u>]	CHRIS [fs] LIKE <u>GOLF</u>. (1x)
<u>To see</u> is <u>to believe</u>. [<u>S</u>, <u>PN</u>]	<u>SEE</u> EQUAL <u>BELIEVE</u>. (1x, 1x)

Stacey and Casey love <u>to cook</u>, <u>swim</u> and <u>play</u> cards.	STACEY [fs], CASEY [fs], TWO-OF-THEM KISS-FIST <u>COOK</u> (2x), <u>SWIM</u> (2x), <u>PLAY</u> (2x) CARD.

Adjective Phrases [Adj Phr] and Adverb Phrases [Adv Phr]

English Note: **Adjective phrases** *and* **adverb phrases** *are formed by adding an intensifier to the adjective or adverb:* "<u>very</u> interesting" [Adj], "<u>a little bit</u> boring" [Adj], "<u>somewhat</u> slowly" [Adv]. *(See discussion of* **Intensifiers** *on p. 43.)*

ASL Note: **Adjectives** *and* **adverbs** *are modified by* <u>intensifying the movement of the noun or verb sign</u> <u>and/or</u> *intensifying the accompanying* <u>facial expression</u>.

ASL Examples:

DEAF CHILD WITH DEAF PARENT++ TEND <u>VERY-SMART</u> (eyebrows scrunched, head forward, lips /mm/).

FOR LIPREAD, DEAF <u>WATCH</u> LIP (eyebrows scrunched, head forward, lips /mm/).

Prepositional Phrases [Prep Phr]

<u>Note:</u> *(See discussion of* **Prepositions** *on pp. 53ff.)*

DECLARATIVE SENTENCE STRUCTURES: Basic English Sentence Patterns

English Note: English has only <u>six</u> basic sentence or clause structures [Cl], *often called "kernels" because they cannot be reduced any further; they can be* <u>expanded</u>, *however, with the addition of auxiliaries, other modifiers, and additional phrases and clauses. The six basic English clause structures are:*

A) Subject - Intransitive Verb [S Vi]

B) Subject - Transitive Verb - Direct Object of the Verb [S Vt DO]

C) Subject - Transitive Verb - Indirect Object of the Verb - Direct Object of the Verb [S Vt IO DO]

D) Subject - Verb "To Be" - Predicate Noun [S Vbe PN]

E) Subject - Linking Verb - Predicate Adjective [S LV PA]

F) "There" - Verb "To Be" - Subject - Adverb ["There" Vbe S Adv]

Each is considered below.

A) <u>Declarative Sentences: Subject - Intransitive Verb:</u> [S Vi]

English-ASL Notes: 1) Declarative sentences make a statement.

2) This clause pattern functions the same in both English and ASL. (See discussion of intransitive verbs on p. 22.)

English	ASL
Birds fly. [S Vi]	BIRD FLY CL:55 (wiggle upward) [S Vi].
Flowers <u>grow</u>. [S Vi]	FLOWER THEY GROW [S Vi].

B) Declarative Sentences: Subject - Transitsive Verb - Direct Object of the Verb [S Vt DO]

English-ASL Note: While English has only one form of this clause pattern, ASL has several. (See discussion of Transitive Verbs on p. 21.)

English	ASL
I <u>love</u> ASL. [S Vt DO]	1) I <u>KISS-FIST</u> ASL. [S VT DO]
	2) I <u>KISS-FIST</u> ASL I. [S VT DO S]
	3) ASL I <u>KISS-FIST</u> [DO S VT]
	4) ASL <u>KISS-FIST</u> I. [DO VT S]
	5) <u>KISS-FIST</u> ASL I. [VT DO S]

C) Declarative Sentences: Subject - Transitive Verb - Indirect Object of the Verb - Direct Object of the Verb [S Vt IO DO]

English Notes: 1) This sentence pattern is a variation of an expanded form of the S Vt DO structure above. The expanded form occurs only with certain verbs that can be followed by an adverbial prepositional phrase [Adv Prep Phr] with "to" or "for."

"To" : GIVE	HAND	LEND	PAY	SEND
SHOW	SING	TEACH	TELL	WRITE
"For": BAKE	BUY	COOK	DRAW	FIX
MAKE	PLAY (music)			

2) The indirect object of the verb **[IO]** *is made when the* object of the preposition "to" or "for" *drops the preposition and moves in* <u>front</u> *of* **the** direct object of the verb **[DO]**. *So the* "indirect object" *comes between the* verb *and its* direct object. *The meaning of the two sentence patterns is exactly the same in English.*

<u>**ASL Note**</u>: *ASL does* <u>not</u> *have this* **indirect object** *structure.*

<u>**English Examples**</u>:

S Vt DO <u>Adv Prep Phr</u>	S Vt <u>IO</u> DO
The boy gave chocolates <u>to his mother</u>.	The boy gave <u>his mother</u> chocolates.
Please tell a story <u>to the children</u>, then bake some cookies <u>for them</u>.	Please tell <u>the children</u> a story, then bake <u>them</u> some cookies.
The young man bought a diamond ring <u>for his fiancée</u>.	The young man bought <u>his fiancée</u> a diamond ring.

D) Declarative Sentences: Subject - Verb "To Be" - Predicate Noun [S Vbe PN]

<u>**English Note**</u>: *The* predicate nominative, *or* predicate noun **[PN]**, *is a* noun structure *or* pronoun *that follows* "To Be" *or* "To Become" **[Vbe]** *and means the same as the* subject **[S]** *of the sentence.*

<u>**ASL Note**</u>: *ASL does* <u>not</u> *have* "To Be," *but it does have* **BECOME.**

English	ASL
My ASL tutor is <u>Randy</u>. [Proper N]	MY ASL TUTOR <u>RANDY</u> [fs].

That black lab became <u>a service dog</u>. [N Phr]	BLACK LAB [fs] DOG-THERE BECOME <u>SERVICE DOG</u> FINISH.

E) Declarative Sentences: Subject - Linking Verb - Predicate Adjective [S LV PA]

<u>English-ASL Note</u>: The function of an adjective is to modify or describe a noun. A predicate adjective describes the subject of a sentence but comes <u>after</u> the linking verb, so is in the <u>predicate</u> part of the sentence.

English	ASL
The flowers smell <u>sweet</u>.	FLOWER THEY SMELL <u>SWEET</u>.
The final exam was <u>easy</u>.	FINAL TEST <u>EASY</u>.
Marty will become <u>rich</u>.	MARTY [fs] WILL BECOME <u>RICH</u>.

F) Declarative Sentences: "There" - Verb "To Be" - Subject - Adverb ["There" Vbe S Adv]

<u>English Note</u>: This clause pattern does <u>not</u> begin with the adverb of place "there." It begins with an idiomatic structure word, "there," plus some tense of the verb "To Be," followed by the subject and any form of an adverb.

<u>ASL Note</u>: This sentence pattern is expressed in Spanish by "hay," in French by "il y a," and in ASL by the existential HAVE.

English	ASL
<u>There are</u> books on the shelf. [Adv Prep Phr]	1) SHELF-THERE <u>HAVE</u> BOOK (CL:BB++→). 2) BOOK++ <u>HAVE</u> SHELF-THERE. 3) <u>HAVE</u> BOOK++ THERE SHELF.
<u>There was</u> a big sale at Macy's last week. [Adv Phr of time]	---------TI--------- LAST-WEEK MACY'S [fs] <u>HAVE</u> BIG #SALE.
<u>There's</u> a fire!	<u>HAVE</u> FIRE!

<u>There is</u> a large crowd at the ASL expo.	ASL EXPO [fs] <u>HAVE</u> PEOPLE CL:Bent 55 wiggle→ R.

Declarative Sentences: Affirmative

English-ASL Note: **Declarative sentences** *that are not in the* **negative** *are in the* <u>*affirmative*</u>*. Since ASL is a visual-spatial language,* <u>*non-verbal behaviors*</u> *are* **critical** *to communicating meaning.* **Affirmative sentences and clauses** *frequently incorporate* <u>*head nodding*</u> *to indicate both affirmation and agreement.*

ASL Notes: *1) Symbol --- Y --- [head nodding]*

English	ASL
	---Y---
Kim can sign ASL.	1) KIM [fs] CAN SIGN ASL.
	------------------Y------------------
	2) KIM [fs] CAN SIGN ASL. (okay for short sentence)

2) *Other common uses of --- Y --- include:*

AGREE	CAN	FINE	KNOW/KNOW-THAT
LIKE	NATURALLY/OF COURSE	OH-I-SEE	#OK
POSSIBLE	RIGHT	SAME/LIKE	SURE/TRUE/REALLY
UNDERSTAND	WANT	YES	#YES

Declarative Sentences: Exclamatory

English-ASL Note: *This situation occurs when someone is excited, surprised, frustrated or angry. The signing increases in intensity as well as speed. Head nodding [---Y---] can be included.*

English	ASL
The San Diego Padres won!	SD PADRES WON!
	------------Y---------
I passed the class!	I PASS CLASS!

He kicked me!   HE KICK ME!

Declarative Sentences: Topicalization (Topic-Comment, etc.)

ASL Notes: 1) Symbol --- T --- [with <u>raised</u> eyebrows and somewhat <u>raised</u> head]

2) In most cases, place the main idea at the <u>beginning</u> of the ASL sentence.

3) There is <u>seldom more than one</u> topic marker in a sentence.

English	ASL
I am a member of the National Association of the Deaf.	---T--- NAD, I MEMBER.

4) <u>Topic</u> indicator takes precedence over <u>time</u> indicator, which can also be placed at the end of a short sentence <u>without non-verbal behaviors/ facial expression</u>.

English	ASL
<u>The World Games of the Deaf</u> took place in Los Angeles <u>in 1985</u>.	----T---- --------TI------- 1) <u>WGD</u>, <u>PAST 1985</u>, HAPPEN THERE LA. ----T---- 2) <u>WGD</u> HAPPEN THERE LA <u>PAST 1985</u>.

INTERROGATIVE SENTENCE STRUCTURES

<u>Interrogative Sentences: Yes/No Questions [Q]</u>

<u>English Notes</u>: 1) To form Yes/No questions, put the auxiliary verb or "To Be" <u>in front of</u> the subject.

English Statement	English Question
You <u>will</u> <u>help</u> me with my research.	<u>Will</u> you <u>help</u> me with my research?

64

I. King Jordan <u>was</u> the first deaf president of Gallaudet University.

<u>Was</u> I. King Jordan the first deaf president of Gallaudet University?

> **2) If there is <u>no</u> auxiliary verb or "To Be," use the appropriate tense of "To Do" in front of the subject. The verb then goes into the infinitive (base) form.**

English Statement	English Question
He now <u>signs</u> fluently.	<u>Does</u> he now <u>sign</u> fluently?
The hearing dog <u>wore</u> an orange jacket.	<u>Did</u> the hearing dog <u>wear</u> an orange jacket?

ASL Note: Symbol --- Q --- [with <u>raised</u> eyebrows, <u>forward</u> or <u>diagonal</u> head, <u>forward</u> shoulders, the last sign <u>held a little longer</u>]

English	ASL
<u>Do</u> you <u>want</u> some ice cream?	--------------------Q-------------------- YOU <u>WANT</u> ICE-CREAM? *(no "To Do")*
<u>Is</u> he deaf?	--------Q------ HE DEAF? *(no "To Be")*
<u>Have</u> they <u>seen</u> a residential school for the deaf?	--------------------------------Q---------------------------- THEY DEAF-SCHOOL <u>TOUCH FINISH</u>? *(no "To Have")*
Do<u>n't</u> you want to go? [neg]	--------------------Q----------------- YOU <u>NOT</u> WANT GO? *(no "To Do"; neg headshake)*

Interrogative Sentences: Wh- Questions [WQ]

ASL Note: Symbol --- WQ --- [with <u>squeezed</u> eyebrows and <u>forward</u> or <u>diagonal</u> head]

HOW	HOW MANY/HOW MUCH	WHAT/WHATEVER
WHEN WHERE WHICH		WHO
whose (ASL WHO'S) WHY/FOR-FOR (ASL only)		WHY-NOT

English-ASL Note: **The interrogative pronoun question words are the same in both English and ASL.**

English-ASL Exceptions: **1) ASL does not have the English interrogative question word "whom," which is the objective form of "who." Informal ASL can use #FOR-FOR instead of WHY.**

2) ASL signs WHO'S for the possessive English interrogative question word "whose."

English	ASL
<u>What</u> time is it?	---------WQ------- 1) <u>WHAT</u> TIME? (TIME tapped 1x on non-dominant hand) --WQ-- 2) TIME? (tapped 2x)
<u>Whose</u> gloves are these?	---WQ---- GLOVES THESE <u>WHO'S</u>?

ASL Notes: **1) If the <u>Wh- word</u> is placed at the beginning, the non-manual marker continues to the end.**

<u>Who</u> was Laurent Clerc?	------------------WQ------------------ 1) <u>WHO</u> LAURENT-CLERC? (hyphen indicates name sign)

2) If the <u>Wh- word</u> is placed at the end, the non-manual marker occurs only at the <u>Wh- word</u>.

--WQ--
2) LAURENT-CLERC <u>WHO</u>?

3) In a <u>double</u> Wh- Question for emphasis, the non-manual marker occurs from beginning to end.

-----------------------WQ-----------------------
3) <u>WHO</u> LAURENT-CLERC <u>WHO</u>?

ASL Exception: **Use <u>raised</u> eyebrows instead in the following situations:**

English	ASL
<u>How</u> are you?	----------Q---------- <u>HOW</u> YOU? (to start a conversation)
<u>Why not</u>?	---------Q--------- 1) <u>WHY NOT</u>? (excitement, <u>not</u> asking for explanation) ----------Q--------- 2) <u>WHY-NOT</u>?
<u>Why</u> don't we go to the movies?	----------------------Q---------------------- <u>WHY NOT</u> WE GO MOVIE? (anticipation)
<u>Who</u> won the game?	----------Q---------- <u>WHO</u> WON? (strong curiosity)
<u>Where</u> did you find it?	----------------Q---------------- <u>WHERE</u> YOU FIND? (excitement)

<u>ASL Notes:</u> *1) If a* **Wh-** *word (interrogative pronoun) is used for a* non-**Wh-Question** *function—such as introducing a noun clause* **[N Cl]**—*it is called a* relative pronoun. *Facial expression remains* <u>neutral</u>.

2) The relative pronoun *"when" is signed* **HAPPEN**, *and "how" is signed by shaking the dominant* **A** *hand that is touching the non-dominant* **A** *hand,* **PO** *center.*

English	ASL
They're wondering <u>where</u> Logan works.	THEY WONDER <u>WHERE</u> LOGAN [fs] WORK. [N Cl]
Father knows <u>what</u> we want.	FATHER KNOW <u>WHAT</u> WE WANT. [N Cl]
You understand <u>why</u> I'm worried.	YOU UNDERSTAND <u>WHY</u> I WORRY. [N Cl]
Tell us <u>how much</u> you need.	TELL-US <u>HOW-MUCH</u> YOU NEED. [N Cl]
I'll get a certificate <u>when</u> I graduate.	I GET CERTIFICATE <u>HAPPEN</u> I GRADUATE. [Adv Cl]

<u>ASL Note:</u> *Some* **Wh-** *words can be* <u>*fingerspelled*</u> *for three purposes: to express* <u>*anger*</u>, <u>*curiosity*</u> *or* <u>*surprise*</u>: **HOW, WHAT, WHEN, WHO** *and* **WHY.**

English	ASL
<u>What</u> did Tyler say? (surprise)	TYLER [fs] SAY <u>WHAT</u> [fs]?
<u>Why</u> did you lie to me? (anger)	YOU LIE ME <u>WHY</u> [fs]?
<u>Who</u>? (curiosity)	<u>WHO</u> [fs]?
<u>How</u>?	<u>HOW</u> [fs]?

Interrogative Sentences: Rhetorical Questions [RQ]

<u>ASL Notes:</u> *1) This type of question is used when the signer intends to answer the question immediately. It alerts the listener to expect the specified information from the signer.*

2) Do not overuse; as a general rule, use the RQ only every 25-50 sentences.

3) Symbol --- RQ --- [with <u>raised</u> eyebrows and <u>forward</u> or <u>diagonal</u> head]

English	ASL
I had pancakes for breakfast.	---RQ--- I BREAKFAST <u>WHAT</u>? PANCAKE [fs].
Las Vegas is in the desert.	----RQ---- LV <u>WHERE</u>? DESERT.

*4) Many ASL users sign **HOW** or **WHY** in the RQ mode for "because" or "due to."*

English	ASL
Tracy became deaf from a bout with spinal meningitis.	---RQ--- TRACY [fs] BECOME DEAF <u>HOW</u>? SPINAL MENINGITIS [fs].
Mother did not come <u>because</u> she was sick.	---RQ--- MOTHER NOT COME, <u>WHY</u>? SHE SICK.
The game was canceled <u>due to</u> rain.	---RQ--- GAME CANCEL, <u>WHY</u>? RAIN.

*5) Although the rhetorical question most often deals with **Wh-**question words, it can also be used for **Yes/No** questions.*

English	ASL
Do I want to go? <u>Yes</u>, I want to go.	---------RQ--------- --Y-- WANT GO I? <u>YES</u>, I WANT GO.
Was your research on Helen Keller good? <u>As always!</u>	-----------------------RQ---------------------- YOUR RESEARCH HK GOOD? ----------Y---------- <u>NATURALLY!</u>
Will we visit Gallaudet University? <u>Absolutely!</u>	--------------------------RQ---------------------------- WE TOUCH GALLAUDET WILL? ----Y---- <u>SURE!</u>
Have I bought a new van? <u>No, not yet.</u>	-----------RQ------------ I BUY NEW VAN [fs]? -----------N---------- <u>NO, NOT-YET.</u>

Interrogative Sentences: Tag Questions

<u>*English-ASL Note:*</u> *Tags are little questions tacked onto the end of a declarative sentence. Spanish and French use "verdad?" and "n'est pas?" respectively. ASL uses TRUE? or a wiggled [X++] with <u>raised</u> eyebrows and <u>forward</u> or <u>diagonal</u> head. Also ASL and English both use "right?"*

English	ASL
They're deaf, <u>huh</u>?	----Q---- 1) THEY DEAF, <u>RIGHT?</u> ----Q---- 2) THEY DEAF, <u>TRUE?</u> ---Q--- 3) THEY DEAF [<u>x++</u>]? (wiggled)

<u>*English Notes:*</u> *1) Other tag endings in English are more complicated in their construction. The general rules are:*

1) If there is an auxiliary verb or the verb "To Be" in the declarative statement, use it in the <u>same</u> tense, add the /-n't/ suffix and repeat the appropriate pronoun for the subject antecedent.

<u>*English Examples:*</u>

Statement	Tag Question
Billie and Bobbie <u>are</u> hard of hearing.	Billie and Bobbie <u>are</u> hard of hearing, <u>aren't they?</u>

The interpreter <u>could</u> sign well.   The interpreter <u>could</u> sign well, <u>couldn't he</u>?

2) *If there is <u>no</u> auxiliary verb or the verb "To Be," use the appropriate tense of the auxiliary "To Do."*

Statement	Tag Question
That deaf professor teaches ASL.	That deaf professor teaches ASL, <u>doesn't she</u>?
You ordered video relay service.	You ordered video relay service, <u>didn't you</u>?

3) *If the statement is in the negative, do <u>not</u> add /-n't/.*

Statement	Tag Question
Our old TV <u>didn't</u> have captions.	Our old TV <u>didn't</u> have captions, <u>did it</u>?
Jesse and Sandy <u>won't</u> go to a mainstreamed school next year.	Jesse and Sandy <u>won't</u> go to a mainstreamed school next year, <u>will they</u>?

DEPENDENT CLAUSES [Cl]

Noun Clauses [N Cl]

<u>English Notes</u>: **1)** **Noun clauses** *function as* **Subject [S], Direct Object of the Verb [DO], Predicate Noun [PN]** and **Object of the Preposition [OP],** *but <u>not</u> as* **Indirect Object of the Verb.**

2) **Noun clauses** *are introduced by* relative pronouns: "that," "who(ever)," "whom(ever)," "whose," "which(ever)," "where(ever)."

<u>ASL Notes</u>: **1)** **ASL does <u>not</u> always use a** relative pronoun.

2) **ASL does <u>not</u> have the** relative pronouns "whom(ever)" or "whose."

English	ASL
<u>How the police solved the crime</u> was fascinating. [S]	----------------------T---------------------- <u>HOW POLICE SOLVE CRIME</u> [fs], FASCINATING.
The deaf clients felt <u>that the interpreters were not prepared</u>. [DO]	-----------T----------- DEAF CLIENT THEY FEEL <u>INTERPRETER</u> -----------N---------- <u>NOT PREPARE</u>.

70

English	ASL
The teacher tested the students on <u>what they had learned</u>. [OP]	TEACHER TEST STUDENT ABOUT <u>THEY LEARN SINCE</u>.
This book's exactly <u>what we need</u>! [PN]	THIS BOOK EXACT <u>WE NEED</u>!

Adjectival Clauses [Adj Cl]

English Notes: 1) Adjective clauses can modify any noun, no matter what its function in the sentence: Subject [S], Direct Object of the Verb [DO], Predicate Noun [PN], *and* Object of the Preposition [OP], *but not as* Indirect Object of the Verb.

2) Adjective clauses *are introduced by* relative pronouns: "that," "what(ever)," "who(ever)," "whose," "which(ever)," "where(ever)."

*ASL Note: ASL does not use "whose"/*WHO'S *as a relative pronoun, only as an interrogative pronoun.*

English	ASL
The restaurant <u>where Dusty works</u> has good food. [modifies S]	RESTAURANT <u>WHERE DUSTY [fs]</u> <u>WORK</u> HAVE GOOD FOOD.
The video relay service <u>that Joey uses</u> is the best. [modifies S]	---------T--------- <u>VRS JOEY USE</u>, BEST.
Our class will visit Canine Companions for Independence, <u>which trains service dogs</u>. [modifies DO]	OUR CLASS WILL VISIT CCI <u>THAT</u> <u>TRAIN SERVICE DOG</u>.
<u>Wherever I go</u>, my kitten follows me. [S]	------------CC----------- <u>WHEREVER I GO</u>, MY BABY CAT FOLLOW ME.

Adverbial Clauses [Adv Cl]

English-ASL Notes: 1) Adverbial clauses [Adv Cl] modify the verb, *telling how, how often, how much, when, where and why the action takes place.*

2) *An adverbial clause begins with an* adverbial conjunction, *also called a* subordinating conjunctions, *because it introduces a* subordinate (or dependent) clause.

3) [*] indicates that **ASL** *shares these adverbial conjunctions* **with** *English.*

*after	*although	as	*as [fs] long (as)	*as [fs] soon (as)
because (of)	*before	*even if	*even though	*if
in order that	*in spite of the fact that	now that	once	*since
*so (that)	*suppose	though	unless	*until
*when(ever)	*where(ever)	whether (or not)		*while

Adverbial Clause: Conditional

<u>*ASL Notes*</u>*: 1) Symbol* --- **CC** --- [with <u>raised</u> eyebrows]

2) With any conditional adverbial conjunction, generally place the conditional clause at the <u>beginning</u> of the sentence.

3) If the adverbial conjunction "when" is used to introduce an adverb clause, "when" is signed **HAPPEN.**

English	ASL
I learned ASL <u>when I was seven.</u>	----------------CC----------------- HAPPEN I OLD SEVEN, I LEARN ASL.
<u>If you know two languages,</u> you are bilingual.	---------------------------CC------------------------ IF YOU KNOW TWO LANGUAGE, YOU BILINGUAL [fs].
<u>Once he landed in England,</u> Rev. Thomas Gallaudet traveled widely.	--------------CC------------- ARRIVE ENGLAND, GALLAUDET TRAVEL++.
<u>Had I known about it,</u> I would have come.	-------------CC------------ IF I KNOW-THAT, I come.

| If so, then you . . . . | ---CC-- |
| | 1) <u>IF YES</u>, YOU . . . . |

2) (No "if" sign, <u>head up, raised eyebrows</u>)
-CC-
<u>YES</u>, YOU . . . . (head and eyebrows normal).

Adverbial Clause: Time

ASL Notes: 1) *Symbol --- TI ---*

2) *Once a time frame is established (past, present or future), it is assumed to remain the same for all the following sentences until a new time is established.*

3) *When a sentence contains a time-sensitive sequence, place the adverbial clause toward the <u>end</u> of the sentence; do <u>not</u> raise eyebrows.*

English	ASL
I will keep eating <u>until I am full</u>.	I EAT-CONTINUOUS <u>UNTIL I FULL</u>.
Please stay <u>as long as you can</u>.	PLEASE STAY <u>AS LONG POSSIBLE</u>.
My dad had a driver's license for 52 years <u>before he died</u>.	MY DAD HAVE DRIVE LICENSE 52 YEAR <u>BEFORE HE DIE</u>.
Many warships were docked together in 1941 <u>when Japan attacked Pearl Harbor</u>.	---------TI------- <u>BACK 1941</u>, MANY WAR SHIP PARK CL:3-in-a-ROW <u>HAPPEN JAPAN BOMB PEARL HARBOR</u> [fs].
I want to know <u>when my boss calls</u>.	I WANT KNOW <u>HAPPEN MY BOSS TTY-ME</u>.

SECTION THREE:
LEXICALIZED STRUCTURES

FINGERSPELLING [fs]

Fingerspelling: Numbers

ASL Notes: 1) Sign <u>cardinal numbers</u> *1-5 and 11-15 with* palm orientation [PO] <u>inward</u>; *sign the rest with* **PO** <u>forward</u>. *Sign any* <u>range</u> *of these numbers with* **PO** *respectively inward or forward: 3 - 5* **YEAR** *=* **PO** <u>inward</u>; *25 - 30* **YEAR** *=* **PO** <u>forward</u>.

English	ASL
My apartment address is <u>395</u> Maple St.	MY #APT ADDRESS <u>3-9-5</u> (PO forward) MAPLE [fs] ST.
The emergency phone number is <u>911</u>.	EMERGENCY PHONE NUMBER <u>9-1-1</u>. (PO forward)
The dentist's office is number <u>26</u>.	DENTIST OFFICE DOOR NUMBER <u>26</u>. (PO forward)
<u>Two</u> times <u>two</u> equals <u>four</u>.	<u>2</u> MULTIPLY <u>2</u> EQUAL <u>4</u>. (all PO forward)

2) Sign **THOUSAND** *for quantity only.*

English	ASL
1800 ("eighteen hundred") chickens	1) ONE <u>THOUSAND</u> 800 CHICKEN (signed) 2) 1,800 CHICKEN (written)

3) For <u>ordinal numbers</u>, *twist 1st through 9th. Starting with 10th, sign the number once, then add a fingerspelled /–TH/, except for numbers ending in 1, 2, or 3 when part of a sign, title, or address: "22**<u>ND</u>** INTERSECTION 3<u>RD</u> AVE."*

4) "Rule of 9" for time concepts (seconds, minutes, hours, days, weeks, months and years): Numbers can always be fingerspelled separately from the signed time concept (11 MONTH, 25 YEAR), but can also be <u>embedded</u> *for the numbers* <u>1-9</u>.

ASL Exception: _The number_ _10_ _can be imbedded (on the top of the dominant index finger only, not on the non-dominant palm) for_ _age_, _dollars_, _cents_ _and_ _minutes_ _only._

English	ASL
We work <u>eight hours</u> a day.	1) WE WORK <u>8 [fs]</u> <u>HOUR</u> EVERYDAY. 2) WE WORK <u>8-HOUR [embedded]</u> EVERYDAY.
School is closed for <u>two weeks</u>.	1) SCHOOL CLOSE <u>2 [fs]</u> <u>WEEK</u>. 2) SCHOOL CLOSE <u>2-WEEK [embedded]</u>.
There are <u>twelve months</u> in a year.	ONE YEAR HAVE <u>12 [fs]</u> MONTH.
I'll meet you in <u>ten minutes</u>.	1) I-MEET-YOU <u>10 [fs]</u> <u>MINUTE</u>. 2) I-MEET-YOU <u>10-MINUTE [embedded]</u>.

Fingerspelling: Years

English-ASL Note: _The years before 2000 are signed and pronounced the same in both English and ASL: "1987" = "nineteen eighty-seven."_

ASL Note: _For the years 2000 and beyond, do_ _not_ _sign_ **THOUSAND** _in the year._

English	ASL
2004 (two <u>thousand</u> four)	1) 2004 [2-0-0-4 fs] 2) 04
2015 (two thousand fifteen/ twenty-fifteen)	20-15 (move each number 1x)
1) In eighteen years 2) Eighteen years from now	<u>18</u> YEAR <u>FUTURE</u> (move "18" 1x before the noun)

Fingerspelling: Months of the Year

ASL Notes: 1) *The seven months with long names are abbreviated in fingerspelling:* JAN, FEB, AUG, SEPT, OCT, NOV *and* DEC. *No periods are used as this would force the sign to be circled incorrectly.*

2) *The five months with short names are spelled out in full:* MARCH, APRIL, MAY, JUNE *and* JULY.

Fingerspelling: Age

English	ASL
Shea is <u>eight years old</u>.	1) SHEA [fs] <u>OLD 8</u>. 2) SHEA [fs] <u>OLD-8</u>.
Our daughter is <u>seventeen</u>.	OUR DAUGHTER <u>OLD 17</u>. (move "17" 1x or more)

ASL Note: Display numbers 1-9 with palm orientation <u>forward</u> for both <u>age</u> and <u>time</u> as well as for <u>addresses</u>, <u>telephone numbers</u> and <u>room numbers</u>.

Fingerspelling: Height

ASL Note: For reporting the height of both a person and track meet high jump scores, sign with palm orientation [PO] <u>inward</u>. Move inches <u>sideways</u> (to dominant side): MY SON HEIGHT 6'5"; TODAY HE JUMP 6'8".

Fingerspelling: Abbreviations

ASL Note: The fingerspelled letter with the period is moved in a circle. No periods are used in abbreviated words, with the exception of "the <u>U.S.</u>" and an initialized middle name: Edward <u>M.</u> Gallaudet.

ASL Exception: Do <u>not</u> circle the hand while fingerspelling <u>Mr.</u>, <u>Mrs.</u> or <u>Dr.</u>

English	ASL
My Riverside friend hopes to go to <u>NTID</u>.	MY RIVERSIDE FRIEND HOPE GO <u>NTID</u>.
Two generations of that deaf family have gone to <u>ASDB</u>.	TWO GENERATION DEAF FAMILY GO <u>ASDB</u>.

ASL Note: **NTID** = *National Technical Institute for the Deaf in New York;*
ASDB = *Arizona School for the Deaf and the Blind.*

Fingerspelling: Loan Signs

ASL Notes: *1) There are about 85 signs borrowed from English that involve modified fingerspelling: deleted letters; change in palm orientation, location or movement; circled, twisted or duplicated hand movement.*

2) Loan signs are indicated in gloss by the pound sign [#].

#3D	#ALL	#APT	#BACK	#BALL (baseball call)
#BANK	#BEACH	#BIG	#BS	#BUS
#BUSY	#BUT	#CAB	#CAN	#CAR
#CLUB	#CO(mpany)	#COOL (slang)	#COZY	#DID
#DO-DO	#DOG	#DOING	#DOZ	#EARLY
#EASY	#EEK	#EMAIL	#EX-	#FAV
#FAX	#FIX	#FUN	#GAS	#GO
#HA-HA	#HELL	#HILL	#HOURS	#HURT
#IF	#IND (Indiana)	#JOB	#JV (jr varsity)	#KILL
#KO	#NG (no good)	#NO	#NM (New Mexico)	#MAD
#M-F (Mon-Fri)	#MO (Missouri)		#OFF	#OH
#OIL	#OK	#OR	#OWN	#REF
#SALE	#SEX	#SO	#SOON	#STAR
#STIFF	#STYLE	#SURE	#TAX	#TB (too bad)
#THAT'S ALL	#TOY	#TRUCK	#TV	#UPSET
#VEG	#VR (Voc Rehab)	#WELL	#WHAT	#WHEN
#WILL	#WOULD	#WOW	#YES	#ZZ (pizza)

BOUNCE/REPEAT FAST: #BANK, #DO-DO *(PO upward)*, #DOG, #DID, #HA, #IF

CIRCLE HAND: #EARLY, #OH, #OWN, #SALE *(counter-clockwise)*

DELETE LETTERS: #BANK, #BEACH, #CLUB, #DOING, #DOZ, #EMIL/EIL, #FAV, #JOB, #TRUCK, #WOULD, #YES

DIRECTIONAL: #ALL, #BACK, #GO, #OFF, #TB

FROM DOWNWARD, SNAP UPWARD: #APT, #BANK, #IND, #NG, #STYLE *(down on "y," up on "l")*, #YES

SLIDE TO DOMINANT SIDE: #BS, #CO, #M-F *(PO upward)*, #MAD, #STAR, #STIFF, #WOW

SNAP DOWNWARD: #BALL, #BANK, #BS, #DID *(then upward)*, #EASY, #FUN, #GAS, #KO, *(move to non-dominant side on "STA," dominant side on "R")*, #TOY

SNAP FORWARD: #3D *(PO inward)*, #BIG, #BUS, #BUT, #CAB, #CAN, #CAR, #COOL, #EEK, #HELL, #HILL, #IF, #KILL, #NO, #OIL, #OK, #OR, #REF, #SO, #SOON, #SURE, #TB *(PO upward)*, #THAT'S *(A on B palm)* #ALL, #TRUCK, #TV, #UPSET *(snap forward on "UP," then normal for "SET")*, #WELL, #WILL, #WOW, #YES

TWIST INWARD TO FORWARD: #EASY, #GAS, #HOURS, #HURT, #NM, #NO, #MO, #OWN, #SO, #VR

TWIST FORWARD TO INWARD: #EX, #FAX, #FIX, #JOB, #JV, #NG, #SEX, #TAX, #VEG, #WHAT, #WHEN

Z-SHAPE MOVEMENT: #BUSY, #ZZ

English	ASL
The TTY is <u>not any good</u>.	TTY <u>#NG</u>.
You did an outstanding <u>job</u>.	YOU OUTSTANDING <u>#JOB</u>.
<u>What can I do?</u>/<u>What did I do?</u>	-----WQ----- I <u>#DO-DO</u>?

3) The pound sign is <u>not</u> used for spelling proper nouns. They are fingerspelled normally.

Fingerspelled "IT"

ASL Examples:

DO <u>IT</u>.	FORGET <u>IT</u>.	GO FOR <u>IT</u>.
LOVE <u>IT</u>.	MAKE <u>IT</u>.	THAT('s) <u>IT</u>.
WORTH <u>IT</u>.		

ASL Note: **The English filler subject "it" is discarded in commonly used phrases.**

English	ASL
Take <u>it</u> easy.	1) TAKE EASY. 2) TAKE-EASY.
<u>It</u>'s Friday.	TODAY FRIDAY.
<u>It</u> is important to study.	IMPORTANT STUDY.
<u>It</u> figures.	THAT EXPLAIN.
<u>It</u>'s a good idea.	GOOD IDEA.
I will take care of <u>it</u>.	I WILL TAKE-CARE (careful).

VOCABULARY

Vocabulary: Compound Words

ASL Note: **In most cases, the repetitive movement is reduced to a one-time movement for the first part of the compound sign. Examples:**

BIRD BRAIN (1x, 1x)	BOOKCASE (1x, fs)	BOOKSTORE (1x, 2x)
BOY (and) GIRL (1x, 1x)	BOY SCOUT (1x, 1x)	BUTTERMILK (1x, 1x)
COWBOY (1x, 1x)	EGGPLANT (1x, 1x/fs)	HANDMADE (2x, 2x)
HOMEMADE (2x, 1x)	HOMEWORK (1x, 1x/2x)	LADIES-GENTLEMEN (1x,1x)
LADYBUG (fs, 2x)	LIGHTHOUSE (1x, 1x)	MILKSHAKE (1x or 2x, ++)
PEANUT BUTTER (1x, 1x)	PLAYGROUND (1x, 1x)	SELF-CONSCIOUS (1x, 2x)
SELF-CONFIDENT (1x, 1x)	SELF-RESEPCT (1x, 1x)	SNOWMAN (++, 1x)
SNOWSHOES (++, 2x)	STARFISH (1x/fs, fs)	WATERMELON (1x, 2x)

Vocabulary: Prefixes

Prefix	Meaning	English	ASL
dis-	not	disapprove	NOT APPROVE, NOT ACCEPT
		disinterested	NEUTRAL
		dissatisfied	NOT SATISFY
en-	change N, Adj to V	endanger	MAKE DANGER
		enable	MAKE ABLE
ex-	former	ex-wife	#EX WIFE
il-	not	illegible	NOT CLEAR
		illegal	NOT LEGAL/FORBIDDEN
im-	not	imbalance	NOT BALANCE/OFF-BALANCE
		impossible	NOT POSSIBLE/IMPOSSIBLE
in-	not	incomplete	NOT FULL, NOT FINISH
		invalid	NOT VALID [fs]/TRUE
ir-	not	irregular	NOT REGULAR
		irresponsible	NOT RESPONSIBLE
mis-	wrong	mismanage	WRONG MANAGE
re-	again	reuse, recycle	AGAIN USE, USE AGAIN

| un- | not | <u>un</u>known | <u>NOT</u> KNOW, <u>UN</u> [fs] KNOW |

Vocabulary: Idiomatic Equivalencies

| 4th of July | JULY 4th |
| 30-day guarantee | ONE-MONTH GUARANTEE/PROMISE |

A

According to	SAY
A couple of days	2-DAY
Abuse	MIND TORTURE; PHYSICAL BEAT; WRONG USE
Admire, love (a thing)	KISS-FIST
All the time	ALWAYS; ALL TIME; #ALL TIME
Already	FINISH
Alzheimer's disease	MIND DIMINISH/MIND ALZ
Anyway/by the way/nevertheless/ nonetheless/whatever	ANYWAY
A piece of paper	ONE PAPER
Apology/apologize	SORRY
Approximate(ly)	ABOUT/AROUND
Armed forces	MILITARY DIFFERENT++ GROUP
Around-the-clock	24 HOUR/ALL-DAY+ALL-NIGHT
As a matter of fact	TRUE/TRUTH; TRUE BUSINESS
As fast as (100 mph)	FAST (100 mph)
Attend a meeting	GO-TO/SHOW-UP MEETING

Attorney	LAWYER
A + W Root Beer	AWRB
A year and a half	1 ½ YEAR

B

Baby shower	EXPECT BABY PARTY
Baked goods	BAKE COOKIE, CAKE, etc.
Because	WHY? [RQ]
Besides, further	PLUS; WHAT MORE; OTHER
Beware of (dog)	WARNING (DOG)
Birth defect	BORN WRONG; WRONG BORN
Bodyguard	PROFESSIONAL/SECRET PROTECTOR
Bold plan	BRAVE PLAN
Bold type	DARK WORD
Book fair	BOOK SALE
Bridal shower	BRIDAL [fs] PARTY; NEW WIFE PARTY
Bright color	STRONG COLOR
Bruise	BLACK/BLUE/PURPLE SPOT
Business fair	BUSINESS INFORMATION TABLE++
By the way	FOR YOUR INFORMATION; MIND POP-UP; NOW NEW TALK

C

Can't stand (it)	CAN'T PUT-UP-WITH; CAN'T BEAR/TOLERATE (THIS)

Chevrolet	CHEV [fs], CHEVY [fs]
City Hall	GOVERNMENT BUILDING
Circumstance	SITUATION
Cold cuts	COLD (SANDWICH) MEAT
Comfort food	HOME COOK FOOD
Complimentary continental breakfast	FREE SMALL BREAKFAST
Composition book	WRITE (1x) BOOK (1x)
Condiments	KETCHUP, MAYO [fs], MUSTARD [fs], etc.
Copier	COPY MACHINE
Count on (someone/something)	DEPEND
County fair	COUNTY FERRIS-WHEEL

D

Deadline	LAST DAY/LAST DAY DUE
Decade	TEN YEAR
Dept of Rehabilitation (DOR)	#VR (Vocational Rehabilitation)
Devil's food cake	CHOCOLATE CAKE
Dishwashing detergent	DISH SOAP
Distinguish	NOTICE/TELL DIFFERENCE
Do the dishes	WASH-DISH
Domestic car	AMERICAN CAR
Dozen	12; #DOZ
Dozens/Scores (of)	MANY/MANY++

Down Under	AUSTRALIA
Draw a conclusion	MAKE DECISION
Dressing room	TRY/CHANGE CLOTHES (1x) ROOM
Drive (someone) crazy	MAKE (SOMEONE) CRAZY
Dry cleaners	DRY CLEAN++
Due to	REASON? [RQ]; WHY? [RQ]
Due upon receipt	DUE/PAY NOW
DVD player	DVD MACHINE

E/F/G

Employer	BOSS (small business); #CO (big business)
Endangered species	SHRINK++ ANIMAL TYPE
ER	EMERGENCY ROOM
Every other day	EVERY-2-DAY++
Fair weather	GOOD WEATHER
Farm stand	FARM STORE
Fair job	SO-SO WORK/#JOB
Fat-free	FAT [fs] NONE
Favorite dish	FAVORITE FOOD
Feminine hygiene	WOMAN THING
Field hockey	GRASS HOCKEY
Fix (lunch)	MAKE/COOK (LUNCH)
Folks	PARENT++; PEOPLE

Former	#EX; PAST
Fortunate	LUCKY
Get real	WAKE-UP; COME-ON
Get well	BECOME BETTER/WELL; IMPROVE
Gonna (be going to)	WILL
Gotta (have to)	MUST
Go well	HAPPEN/PROCEED GOOD
Go wrong	HAPPEN WRONG; MESS-UP
Grammar school	ELEMENTARY SCHOOL

H

Hard-boiled eggs	WATER BOIL EGG
Hard liquor	WHISKEY/ALCOHOL; STRONG LIQUOR
Have a seat	SIT-DOWN
Hearing impaired	DEAF. HARD-OF-HEARING
Hence, thus	#SO
Here we go	PROCEED; WE READY GO
Hold a meeting	HAVE MEETING
Homeless	HOME NONE; WITHOUT HOME
Horse pill	CHA PILL
Hours of operation	OPEN HOUR
Household	FAMILY
Hot pink	STRONG PINK

However	BUT
Humans, human beings	PEOPLE

I/J/K

If one (needs)	IF PERSON/ SOMEONE (NEED)
I'll catch you later; See you around	SEE YOU LATER; SEE-YOU-LATER
In the foreseeable future	NEAR-FUTURE (cheek pulled up)
In the meantime	PROCESS READY; STILL PROCESS; UNTIL
Job fair	JOB OPEN INFORMATION/HELP
Knock it off	FINISH
Known for	FAMOUS FOR

L

Late (friend)	DEAD (FRIEND)
Light color, tea; light rain	WEAK COLOR, TEA; LITTLE-BIT RAIN
Lion's Club	LION CLUB [fs]/#CLUB
Live bait	REAL WORM/BUG
Loaf of bread	BREAD
Locker room	CHANGE CLOTHES (1x) ROOM; LOCK ROOM
Long hours	MANY HOUR
Loved ones	FAMILY

M

Make house calls	GO++ HOUSE
Make (up) the bed	MAKE BED
Many retail outlets	MANY STORE
Merry Christmas	MC; HAPPY CHRISTMAS
Mile-long hot dog	LONG HOT-DOG
Misconduct	BAD/WRONG BEHAVIOR
Moreover/in addition	PLUS
Mother-in-law	MOTHER LAW
Mother's Day	MOTHER DAY
Motorist	DRIVER
My old man	MY FATHER; MY HUSBAND

N/O

Nearly	ALMOST
Never mind	FORGET IT [fs]; DROP-IT; WAVE-NO
No trespassing	DON'T WALK THROUGH
Northern California	NORTH CALIFORNIA
Nothing could be further from the truth	NOT TRUE
Nursery	PLANT STORE; CHILD CARE
Objective (Adj)	NEUTRAL
Obedience school	DOG TRAINING SCHOOL; OBEY SCHOOL

Office visit	APPOINTMENT
Offspring/infant	BABY
One another	EACH-OTHER
Otherwise	#OR
Ounce	OZ
Overcooked	COOK TOO-MUCH; BURN
Overseas	OTHER COUNTRY

P/Q

Passenger	RIDER
Password	SECRET/PRIVATE WORD
Peace of mind	PEACE MIND/MIND PEACE
Pedestrian	WALKER
Pet (cat/dog/horse) treat	PET (CAT/DOG/HORSE) COOKIE
Plain clothes cop	SECRET/COVER-UP COP
Possible/possibility	CAN (2x)
Pre-owned vehicle	USED/OLD CAR
Pre-pay	PAY FIRST
Preschool	SMALL-CHILDREN SCHOOL
Pretty sure	FAIRLY (SO-SO) SURE
Prey	SMALL ANIMAL
Prior to	BEFORE
Produce [N] stand	VEGETABLE, FRUIT STORE
Professional athlete	PRO [fs] ATHLETE

Promote	ENCOURAGE; ADVERTISE; SUPPORT
Public/municipal library	COMMUNITY/CITY LIBRARY
Public School	HEARING SCHOOL
Quarterly magazine	EVERY-3-MONTH MAGAZINE

R

Rates keep falling	NUMBER CONTINUE DECREASE
Record still stands	RECORD STILL HOLD/CONTINUE
Recycle	USE AGAIN
Redhead	RED HAIR; ORANGE HAIR
Red tape	RED TAPE
Refrigerator, fridge	#REF
Regular folks	REGULAR PEOPLE
Run to the (grocery) store	GO (FOOD) STORE
(Run) out of	RUN-OUT

S

St. Patrick's Day	IRISH DAY (adult form); PINCH DAY (child form)
Secret code	SECRET WORD/NUMBER
See you around; catch you later	SEE-YOU LATER; SEE YOU LATER
Shop (N)	STORE
Shredder	SHRED MACHINE
Sibling	BROTHER/SISTER

Side effects	PROBLEM POP-UP
Simultaneous	SAME TIME; TIME-SAME
Single day	ONE-DAY
Single parent	SINGLE MOTHER; SINGLE FATHER
Snack	SMALL FOOD; SNACK [fs]
So does/did (Kim)	(KIM [fs]) SAME THING
Soft drink	SODA-POP
Someday; eventually	FUTURE
Sometime (in the fall)	AROUND (FALL)
Sporting goods	SPORT THING
Stabilize	BECOME STABLE
Stand for	REPRESENT; MEAN
Such as	LIKE/SAME

T

Take place	HAPPEN
Take train	RIDE TRAIN
Ten seasons	TEN YEAR
Tennis shoes/sneakers	RUBBER SHOE++
That's why	THAT-ONE; THAT WHY (1x)
The other day	RECENT
This is for real	TRUE BUSINESS
Ton	2,000 POUND

TP	TOILET PAPER
Traffic school	DRIVE SCHOOL
Treat [V]	TAKE-CARE-OF
Trick-or-treat	TEASE #OR CANDY
Trouble-free	TROUBLE NONE
Troubleshoot	INVESTIGATE; PROBLEM SOLVE
Two dozen	24 (ASL prefers numbers)

U/V

Undercooked	COOK NOT ENOUGH; A-LITTLE COOK
Unfortunately	SAD
Urgent care	DOCTOR NOW; EMERGENCY HOSPITAL
Valentine's Day	HEART DAY
Vehicle	CAR/#CAR
Vending machine	CANDY/FOOD/DRINK MACHINE

W-Z

What is the matter (with you)?	WRONG?++ [WQ 2x]
What went wrong?	WHAT HAPPEN WRONG? WHAT WRONG?
Yes, I do	YES; FOR-SURE
You guys	YOU-ALL (sweep center)

Vocabulary: ASL Abbreviations and Acronyms

ASL	English
A	
A (shake)	Anaheim; arthritis; athletics; average
AA	Alcoholics Anonymous; Affirmative Action; American Airlines; Associate of Arts
AAD	American Annals for the Deaf
ABC	Alphabet
AC	Air conditioner/conditioning
AD	Athletic director
ADA	Americans with Disabilities Act
ADJ	Adjective; adjourn; adjunct
ADM	Administration
ADV	Adverb
AGB, AGBell	Alexander Graham Bell
ALZ	Alzheimer's
ASD	American School for the Deaf; American Society for the Deaf
ASLPI	American Sign Language Proficiency Interview
AT	A+ letter grade
AVO	Avocado
AVT	Auditory Verbal Therapy (oral training)

B

B (shake)	Blue
BA	Bank of America
BA/BS	Bachelor of Arts/Science
BB	Blackboard; bulletin board; Bernard Bragg
BC	Baja California; Before Christ; birth control
BI	Bisexuality
BI-BI	Bilingual-bicultural
BK	Burger King
BM	Bowel movement
BO	Body odor
BT	B+ letter grade

C

C (shake)	Cinnamon; conservative; spices
CAD	California/Colorado Association of the Deaf
CAID	Convention of American Instructors of the Deaf
CC	Credit card; Chamber of Commerce; Church of Christ; closed captioned; country club; cross country; Columbus Colony (famous retirement home for Deaf in Ohio)
CCI	Canine Companions for Independence
CDI	Certified Deaf Interpreter
CF	Center field; captioned film (rarely used now)

CH	Channel
CI	Cochlear implant
CL	Classifier; clause; contact lens
CP	Cerebral palsy
CSD	Community Services for the Deaf
CSDF/CSDR	California School for the Deaf at Fremont/Riverside
CSUN	California State University at Northridge
CT	C+ letter grade
CU	Credit union
CW	Civil War

D

D (shake)	Democrat; Denver; diamond
DA	Disability
DB	Database; decibel
DHH	Deaf and hard of hearing
DIV	Division
DO	Direct object of the verb
DOD	Deaf (child) of Deaf (parents)
DOH	Deaf (child) of hearing (parents)
DQ	Dairy Queen; disqualified/disqualification
DS	Down's syndrome; drug store
DSA	Deaf Seniors of America

DT	D+ letter grade
DVTV	Deaf video TV
DWU	Deaf Women United
DX	Diagnosis

E/F/G

E (shake)	Easter; emergency
ED	Education
F (circle, palm in)	Friday
F (shake)	Furniture; nothing (to it)
FAV/#FAV	Favorite
FB	Facebook; feedback; fullback
FF	99; Fairfield; fast forward; french fries
FL	Freelance
FT	Foot/feet; full time
G (move in a circle)	Guard (sports); guarantee
GA (for TTY)	Go ahead
GAL	Gallon
GLAD	Greater Los Angeles Agency on Deafness
GM	General Motors
GU	Gallaudet University
GUAA	Gallaudet University Alumni Association

H

HC	Handicapped; homecoming
HD	Hard disk/drive; Harley Davidson; high definition
HF	Hall of Fame
HH	Hard of hearing; Honolulu
HI	Hearing impaired
HJ	High jump
HK	Helen Keller; Hong Kong
HLAA	Hearing Loss Association of America
HR	Home run; human resources
HP	Hewlett Packard; horsepower
HQ	Headquarters
HS	High school

I/J/K

I (shake)	Infection; insurance
IEP	Individualized Education Plan
IEP/ITP	Interpreter Education/Training Program
J (shake)	Joint
JB	Jack in the Box
JHS	Junior high school
JR NAD	Junior National Association of the Deaf
JW	Jehovah's Witnesses

K (shake)	Kindergarten; kitchen; kosher

L

L (shake)	Large; liberal (political leaning)
LA	Liberal arts; Los Angeles; Louisiana
LD	Learning disability; long distance
LJ	Long jump
LL	Landlord; Little League; low life
LS	Liberal studies
LT	Lake Tahoe; lieutenant; long term
LV	Las Vegas; low verbal (now used rarely)

M

M (shake)	Medium; mineral
M (circle, palm inward or forward)	Monday
MA	Master of Arts
MAX	Maximum
MB	Mercedes Benz
MC	MasterCard; Master of Ceremonies; Merry Christmas
MH	Motor home
MIN	Minimum; minute
MM	M & M candies; Magic Mountain; Marilyn Monroe
MS	Master of Science; Multiple sclerosis

MW	Microwave; man and wife (now used rarely)

N/O

N (shake)	Neutral
NC	No comment; non-credit; North Carolina
NCI	National Captioning Institute
NB	Notebook
NL	Newsletter
NTID	National Technical Institute for the Deaf
O (shake)	Object (grammar); oxygen
OD	Overdose
OIC	Oh, I see
OJ	Orange juice
OO	Out of order (parliamentary rules)
OT	Overtime
OZ	Ounce

P/Q

P (shake)	Purple
PC	Peace Corps; personal computer; politically correct; postcard
PHD	Doctor of Philosophy; doctorate
PJ	Pajamas
PN	Pneumonia; pronoun; predicate noun

PO	Post office; purchase order
PP	Ping pong; Power Point; prepositional phrase
PSE	Pidgin Signed English
PT	Part time
PV	Pole vault
Q (shake)	Quarter (academic or sports)
QB	Quarterback
QT	Quart

R

R (shake)	Raisin; ready; Republican
RB	Racquetball; root beer; running back
RD	*Reader's Digest*
RE	Real estate
REC	Recreation
REV (War)	Revolutionary (War)
REW	Rewind
RID	Registry of Interpreters for the Deaf
RO	Restraining order
RR	Restroom; rest and recuperation; Rolls Royce
RV	Recreational vehicle
RX	Prescription; medicine

S

S (circle, palm in)	Saturday
S (shake)	Scholarship, Seattle, small; subject (grammar)
SAC	Sacramento
SAL	Salutatorian
SB	Santa Barbara; snack bar; Starbucks
SEC	Second (clock time)
SEE	Signing Exact English
SF	San Francisco; San Fernando; Santa Fe
SK (for TTY)	Stop keying
SL	St. Louis; sick leave
SQ FT	Square foot/feet
SS	Shortstop; Social Security; Sunday school
SSI	Supplemental Security Income
ST	Saint (Francis); street
SW	Software; station wagon
SWCID	Southwest Collegiate Institute for the Deaf

T

T (circle, palm in)	Tuesday
T (shake)	Bathroom; toilet
TA	Teacher's aide/teaching assistant

TB	Tablespoon; Taco Bell; Tampa Bay; tuberculosis
TD	Touchdown
TDD	Telecommunications Device for the Deaf
(T)H (H only, circle, palm in)	Thursday
TJ	Tijuana; Trader Joe's
TM	Trademark
TRS	Telecommunication Relay Service
TSP	Teaspoon
TT	Tenure track
TTY	Teletypewriter
TV	Television

U/V

UI	Unemployment Insurance
UN	United Nations
USADSF	USA Deaf Sports Federation
UV	Ultraviolet
V (shake)	Vanilla; vinegar; vitamin
VAL	Valedictorian
VB	Volleyball
VD	Venereal disease; vitamin D
VET	Veteran; veterinarian
VN	Vietnam

VOL	Volume (sound)
VP	Vice-president; videophone
VRS	Video Relay Service
VW	Volkswagen

W-Z

W (circle, palm in)	Wednesday
WC	Worker's compensation
WFD	World Federation of the Deaf
WH	Warehouse
WM	Wal-Mart
WP	Word processing
WRAD	World Recreation Association of the Deaf
WW	Weight Watchers; whole wheat
WW1, 2	World War I, II
Y (shake)	Yellow
ZZ (combined)	Pizza

Vocabulary: U.S. States, ASL Abbreviations

ASL Notes: 1) States with nationwide recognized name signs:

ALASKA	ARIZONA	CALIFORNIA	COLORADO
HAWAII	NEW MEXICO	NEW YORK	OREGON
TEXAS	UTAH	WASHINGTON	WASHINGTON DC

2) States with the earlier postal abbreviations, prior to the revised abbreviations established in the mid-1980s:

Alabama – ALA	Arkansas – ARK	Connecticut – CONN
Delaware – DEL	Florida – FLA	Georgia – GA
Idaho – IDAHO	Iowa – IOWA	Indiana – #IND
Illinois – ILL	Kansas – KS	Kentucky – KY
Louisiana – LA	Maine – MAINE	Maryland – MD
Massachusetts – MASS	Michigan – MICH	Minnesota – MINN
Mississippi – MISS	Missouri – #MO	Montana – MONTANA
Nebraska – NEB	Nevada – NEV/NEVADA	New Hampshire – NH
New Jersey – NJ	New Mexico – #NM	North Carolina – NC
North Dakota – ND	Ohio – OHIO	Oklahoma – OKLA
Pennsylvania – PA	Rhode Island – RI	South Carolina – SC
South Dakota – SD	Tennessee - TENN	Utah – UTAH
Vermont – VT	Virginia – VA	West Virginia – WEST (sign) VA
Wisconsin – WIS (not WISC)		Wyoming – WYO

CLASSIFIERS [CL]

ASL Notes: 1) **Classifiers are handshapes that represent different categories of nouns (people, buildings, things, animals, etc.). Rather than using the same referent by name over and over, classifiers can function as pronouns. The signer must first identify what is being talked about before using an appropriate classifier.**

2) **Classifiers promote the richness and succinctness of ASL for providing details without using too many words in everyday conversation. They are particularly important for storytelling, poetry and drama.**

3) **Classifiers are useful for _description_, _location_, _movement_, _orientation_ and _pluralization_, all addressed below.**

Description: Shape, Size, Texture, Amount and Length

ASL Examples: 1) **CL:B** *is used to represent anything flat, such as a bed, book, paper or table.*

English	ASL
The <u>encyclopedia set</u> is in alphabetical order.	ENCYCLOPEDIA <u>CL:B</u> (upright, move dom→) ABC ORDER.
Please set up the boss' <u>desk</u> on the right wall.	BOSS DESK, PLEASE SET-UP <u>CL:B</u>-R (PO down).

2) **CL:BB** *is superior to* **CL:G** *and* **CL:L** *(discussed below) for length, size, thickness, etc.*

English	ASL
We will barbecue a <u>long</u> Atlantic salmon.	--------------------T-------------------- ATLANTIC [fs] SALMON [fs] *lchal* <u>CL:BB</u> WE BBQ WILL.
The road has been closed due to <u>heavy</u> snow.	---RQ--- ROAD CLOSE WHY? SNOW *lchal* <u>CL:BB</u>.

3) **CL:C/CC** *represent cans, bottles, thick candles, trash cans or any other cylindrical-shaped objects.*

English	ASL
There is a <u>Pepsi bottle</u> floating in the swimming pool.	SWIMMING POOL [fs] HAVE PEPSI BOTTLE <u>CL:C</u> FLOAT.
Please put this <u>glass of milk</u> on the table.	PLEASE MILK GLASS <u>CL:C</u> (move R→) TABLE.
The <u>trunk</u> of that 20-year-old tree is <u>enormous</u>.	TREE-R NOW OLD 20 *lchal* <u>CL:CC</u>.

English	ASL
What a beautiful <u>tall</u> birthday cake!	BIRTHDAY CAKE /cha/ CL:CC BEAUTIFUL!

4) **CL:F** *is used to represent small round objects like buttons, coins, dots, eyes, etc.*

English	ASL
Excuse me, you have a <u>spot</u> of ketchup <u>on your shirt</u>.	EXCUSE-ME, YOU HAVE KETCHUP YOUR SHIRT <u>CL:F</u>. (show exact location on your own shirt)
Valerie has a <u>fistful of change</u>.	VALERIE [fs] HAVE COIN <u>CL:F</u> (palm down, bounce around non-dominant B hand PO up).
The Oxford shirt has a <u>button-down</u> collar.	OXFORD [fs] SHIRT HAVE <u>CL:F</u> (one L and the other R at collar level).

5) **CL:G** *is used for showing an amount of liquid in or the thickness of an object.*

English	ASL
The book Carey is reading is <u>an inch thick</u>.	CAREY [fs] NOW READ BOOK CL:G.
Do you want <u>thick</u> or <u>thin</u> crust pizza?	YOU WANT PIZZA <u>CL:G (tall)</u>, ----WQ---- <u>CL:G (narrow)</u>, WHICH?
There's only <u>a little oil</u> left in the bottle.	BOTTLE HAVE LEFTOVER #OIL <u>CL:G</u>.

6) **CL:I** *denotes a thin line like string, a marked line, a picture frame, etc.*

English	ASL
Mother hangs wet laundry on the <u>clothesline</u>.	------------T----------- WET CLOTHES MOTHER <u>STRING CL:I</u> HANG <u>CL:Q++</u>.
The nurse has asked you to follow the green <u>line</u> to the office.	NURSE ASK YOU FOLLOW GREEN LINE <u>CL:I</u> OFFICE THERE [ix C].

7) CL:Bent L *functions the same as* **CL:G,** *but it indicates bigger, longer or thicker.*

English	ASL
Every morning I start my day with a <u>big glass</u> of water.	--------------T-------------- EVERY-MORNING I START MY DAY DRINK WATER GLASS <u>CL:Bent L</u>.
There's a <u>huge</u> beetle on the screen door.	------T----- BEETLE [fs] */cha/* <u>CL:Bent L</u> ON SCREEN [fs] DOOR.
Please slice the bread <u>extra-thick</u>.	PLEASE BREAD SLICE */cha/* <u>CL:Bent L</u>.

8) CL:R/RR *is used to represent braids, chains or ropes.*

English	ASL
Cats enjoy climbing a <u>rope</u>.	CAT ENJOY ROPE <u>CL:R</u> CLIMB-UP.
Wendy's red hair is in <u>braids</u>.	WENDY [fs] HAVE RED <u>CL:RR</u>.

9) CL:X *is used to represent a bird's beak, coat hanger, hook or person with a bent back or jogging.*

English	ASL
The hawk's <u>hooked beak</u> is for tearing meat.	HAWK [fs] HAVE BEAK <u>CL:X</u> FOR MEAT TEAR.
Meredith's <u>hangers</u> are all in neat order.	MEREDITH [fs] HANGER <u>CL:X</u> NEAT ORDER #ALL.

Location: Near and Far, Left and Right, Front and Back

ASL Examples: 1) **CL:1** *is used to represent a pencil, person, stick, or anything oblong and vertical or horizontal.*

English	ASL
The <u>mailman</u> walked right past my house.	----------T--------- MY HOUSE-L, MAILMAN <u>CL:1</u> WALK (move R to L in front of house).
<u>The candle</u> is in the center of the table.	--------T-------- Table CL:B, CANDLE <u>CL:1</u> (C).
The <u>boy</u> enters stage left and the <u>girl</u> stage right.	-----T----- STAGE, BOY <u>CL:1</u> (move L hand C →), GIRL <u>CL:1</u> (move R hand C ←).

2) **CL:3** *is used to represent any land or water vehicle: boat, bus, car, train, truck, etc.*

English	ASL
The yellow <u>van turned left</u>.	YELLOW VAN [fs] <u>CL:3-TURN-L</u>.
There's a Harley Davidson <u>parked</u> outside.	HD MOTORCYCLE <u>PARK-CL:3</u> OUTSIDE.

3) **CL:Bent 5** *is used to represent a round object: apple, ball, egg, ornament, etc.*

English	ASL
There is an <u>apple</u> on the teacher's desk.	TEACHER DESK CL:B HAVE APPLE <u>CL:Bent 5</u>.
Skippy has a <u>golf ball</u> in his pocket.	SKIPPY [fs] HAVE GOLF BALL <u>CL:Bent 5-POCKET</u>.

4) CL:ILY *is used specifically for aircraft.*

English	ASL
An American Airlines <u>plane</u> is waiting for take-off.	AA PLANE <u>CL:ILY</u> WAIT (non-dom hand) TAKE-OFF (dom hand).
Piper Cub planes are <u>all along that row</u>.	PIPER [fs] PLANE <u>PARK-CL:ILY-sweep R</u>.
My plane is <u>parked on the left</u>.	--------T-------- MY PLANE <u>CL:ILY</u> PARK-LEFT.

5) CL:Bent V *represents a person or an animal that is sitting.*

English	ASL
The five-year-old boy is walking up to <u>Santa Claus in his chair</u>.	SANTA-CLAUS <u>CL:Bent V</u>, BOY OLD 5 CL:1-approach.
The <u>cat is sitting</u> by the window.	WINDOW-R, CAT <u>SIT CL:Bent V</u>.

6) CL:Open A *is used to represent buildings or large objects, like an overstuffed chair or a statue.*

English	ASL
Some people don't like to live in <u>cookie-cutter housing</u>.	SOME PEOPLE DON'T-LIKE LIVE HOUSE <u>CL:Open A++</u> ALL-SAME.
There are several rats' nests <u>scattered</u> throughout the canyon.	CANYON HAVE SEVERAL RAT NEST [fs] <u>CL:Open A++ AROUND</u>.

7) CL:^^ *(upside down V V) is used to represent four-legged animals standing or lying down.*

English	ASL
My <u>corgi</u> is standing right next to me.	CORGI [fs] <u>CL:^^</u> NEXT-TO-ME.
A male elk is watching his herd.	------------T------------ Male elk-R CL:^^ his herd-L look-at++.

Movement: Stationary, Speed and Direction

ASL Examples: 1) **CL:55** (wiggled fingers) *is used to represent foot traffic (people or animals), stampedes, rivers, etc.*

English	ASL
After the game, the fans <u>flowed out</u> of the stadium in <u>all directions</u>.	GAME FINISH, PEOPLE <u>CL:55 (wiggle outward-L and -R)</u>.
The cattle are <u>heading back</u> to the barn.	-------T----- BARN-R, CATTLE <u>CL:55 (wiggle-R)</u>.

Orientation: Arrangement of Objects or Persons

ASL Examples: 1) **CL:Open A** (PO center) *represents buildings or large objects, like a cookie jar, table lamp, storage shed, etc.*

English	ASL
A car dealer likes to have his <u>storefront</u> near the freeway.	CAR DEALER LIKE BUSINESS <u>CL:A</u> FRONT FREEWAY.
Saint Patrick <u>established</u> 300 churches <u>all</u> over Ireland.	SAINT PATRICK [fs], IRELAND, 300 CHURCH SET- UP <u>CL:A++ (2 hands, alternating, move around signing area)</u>.

2) **CL:Bent V** *is used to represent chair arrangement.*

English	ASL
In the deaf education classroom, the <u>desks</u> are <u>arranged in a horseshoe</u>.	----------------------------T---------------------------- DEAF EDUCATION CLASSROOM, DESK <u>CL:Bent V</u> (2h);1) <u>move both hands toward signer starting in the middle of the semicircular set-up</u>; 2) <u>start hands together, then move dominant hand in semicircular set-up</u>.
Ben, who has low vision, <u>sits in front of the teacher</u>.	TEACHER-L, BEN [fs] LOW VISION <u>SIT</u> <u>CL: Bent V-L</u> FRONT.

Pluralization: Singular or Plural

ASL Examples: **1) CL:2, 3, 4 and 5** _denote this number of upright people or animals._

English	ASL
<u>Three</u> Marines are marching with flags.	MARINE <u>CL:3-MARCH</u> WITH FLAG.
<u>Four</u> students need to see me.	STUDENT <u>CL:4-approach-me</u> NEED.

2) CL:3 (horizontal, PO center) _represents land and water vehicles, such as automobiles, bicycles, snowmobiles or boats._

English	ASL
The showroom has <u>a row of new cars</u>.	SHOWROOM HAVE NEW CAR <u>CL:3++</u> <u>(move R→)</u>.
The two brothers <u>raced their bikes up</u> <u>and down the hills.</u>	TWO BROTHER RACE BICYCLE <u>CL:3 (2</u> <u>hands moving up and down appropriately</u>).

3) CL:Bent 55++ (moving outward) _is used to represent a large crowd or a large amount of something._

English	ASL
There is a <u>huge crowd</u> at the beach today.	------TI----- TODAY BEACH HAVE PEOPLE <u>CL:Bent</u> <u>55++</u>.
Every June we get an <u>army of ants</u>.	EVERY-YEAR JUNE WE HAVE ANT <u>CL:Bent 55++</u>.

4) CL:V *can represent either two persons or one person upside-down.*

English	ASL
<u>Two actors</u> will meet me after rehearsal for a discussion.	---------------TI--------------- AFTER REHEARSE, TWO ACTOR <u>CL:V</u> approach-me FOR DISCUSS.
For health reasons, some people do <u>headstands</u>.	FOR HEALTH REASON, SOME PEOPLE head-on-floor <u>CL:V</u>.

SECTION FOUR:
NON-MANUAL BEHAVIORS

GRAMMATICAL FACIAL EXPRESSIONS

ASL Note: In addition to the manual signs themselves, movements of the head, eyes, eyebrows, shoulders or mouth can change the meaning of a sign; they also indicate syntactical structure (a question or command, e.g.)

Facial Expressions: Affirmation

ASL Notes: 1) *Symbol --- Y ---*

2) *Head nodding; smile (sometimes)*

ASL Examples:

```
   ---Y---
YOU CAN.
```

```
-----------Y-----------
FINE WITH ME.
```

3) *Affirmative sign options include:*

AGREE
ALL-RIGHT
NATURALLY
OF COURSE/SURE/TRUE
OH-I-SEE
#OK
RIGHT
YES/#YES

Facial Expressions: Negation

Note: See negative sign options on p. 44.

ASL Notes: 1) *Symbol --- N ---*

2) *Squeezed eyebrows; headshake; sometimes a grimace.*

ASL Examples:

```
 ----N----
```
I <u>CAN'T</u> GO.

```
   -----N----
```
THEY <u>NEVER</u> CALL.

Facial Expressions: Yes/No Questions

<u>Note</u>: See discussion on p. 63.

*<u>ASL Notes</u>: 1) Symbol --- **Q** ---*

> *2) <u>Raised</u> eyebrows; slightly <u>forward</u> or <u>diagonal</u> head; direct eye contact with person being asked*

<u>ASL Examples</u>:

```
------------Q--------------
```
<u>YOU DEAF YOU</u>?

```
----------------------Q----------------------
```
<u>ASL CLASS MEET TIME 1:00</u>?

Facial Expressions: Wh- Questions

<u>Note</u>: (See discussion on p. 64.)

*<u>ASL Notes</u>: 1) Symbol --- **WQ** ---*

> *2) <u>Squeezed</u> eyebrows; slightly <u>forward</u> or <u>diagonal</u> head; direct eye contact with person being asked*

<u>ASL Examples</u>:

```
                   ----WQ----
```
SHAWN [fs] CODA, SODA, <u>WHICH</u>?

```
                              ---------WQ---------
```
NEW ASL FINGERSPELLING BOOK COST <u>HOW-MUCH</u>?

Facial Expressions: Rhetorical Questions

Note: (See discussion on p. 67.)

ASL Notes: 1) Symbol --- RQ ---

> *2) Raised eyebrows for question, then normal for response; slightly forward or diagonal head; direct eye contact with person being asked*

ASL Examples:

```
                    -----------RQ--------
NEW ASL FINGERSPELLING BOOK COST HOW-MUCH? NINETY-FIVE DOLLAR.
```

```
                    ----RQ----
OUR RESEARCH REPORT DUE WHEN? NEXT-WEEK THURSDAY.
```

Facial Expressions: Topic Marker (Topicalization)

Note: (See discussion on p. 63.)

ASL Notes: 1) Symbol --- T ---

> *2) Raised eyebrows; sometimes raised head*

ASL Examples:

```
------------T-----------          ----N-----
RID MEETING, TRACY [fs] CAN'T GO.
```

```
------------------------T-------------------------
MY HUSBAND, I, TWO-OF-US MEET DEAF BOWLING.
```

Facial Expressions: Time Marker

Note: (See discussion on p. 72.)

ASL Notes: 1) Symbol --- TI ---

> *2) Raised eyebrows when time-sensitive indicator is at the beginning of the sentence*

ASL Examples:

```
-------------TI-------------
```
BACK YEAR 1880, DEAF AMERICAN ESTABLISH NAD.

```
------TI------
```
SUMMER, LET'S TAKE-UP DEAF CULTURE CLASS.

Facial Expressions: Conditional Clauses

Note: (See discussion on pp. 71ff.)

ASL Notes: 1) Symbol --- **CC** ---

   2) **Raised** eyebrows when conditional clause is at the **beginning** of the sentence

ASL Examples:

```
---------------------------------------------------------CC-----------------------------------------------------------
```
WHEN STUDENT GRADUATE INTERPRETER EDUCATION PROGAM, SCHOOL GIVE CERTIFICATE.

```
                         ----CC----
```
I ALLERGIC LOBSTER. IF I EAT, I VOMIT.

MOUTH MORPHEMES

English-ASL Note: A morpheme is a portion of a word that makes a difference in the meaning. For English, morphemes are primarily roots, prefixes, and suffixes: "happy" ~ "unhappiness." For ASL, morphemes are facial expression, mouth movements, eye gaze, head tilt, body position, etc.

Note: For additional work on mouth morphemes, see the author's DVD, **Mouth Morphemes in American Sign Language** (1996), Rio Rancho, NM: DeBee Communications.

ASL Note: There are more than 100 different mouth movements in ASL that replace or complement English adjectives and adverbs. Below are some of the most common mouth morphemes:

BEGINNING LEVEL

/cha/: large/long size, tall height, voluminous

English	ASL
Lin and Li want <u>large</u> iced teas.	LIN [fs], LI [fs] WANT <u>LARGE</u> */cha/* TEA COLD.
Our new high school basketball player is <u>super tall</u>.	OUR NEW HS BASKETBALL PLAYER <u>TALL</u> */cha/*, WOW!

/cheek pulled up on one side/: a little bit, near by, recent

English	ASL
Terry <u>hardly</u> works	TERRY [fs] WORK <u>LITTLE-BIT</u> */cheek pulled up/*.
The rain <u>just now</u> stopped.	<u>RECENT</u> */cheek pulled up/* RAIN STOP.

/eek/: despise, dislike, hate

English	ASL
Uncle Todd <u>dislikes</u> raw onion.	UNCLE TODD [fs] <u>DISLIKE</u> */eek/* RAW [fs] ONION.
Many drivers <u>hate</u> the long wait at a red light.	MANY DRIVER <u>HATE</u> */eek/* LONG WAIT RED LIGHT.

/fish/: finish, stop it

English	ASL
<u>Stop it</u>! <u>Knock it off</u>!	<u>STOP-IT</u> */fish/*!
I am <u>through</u> with my homework.	--------------T------------- MY HOMEWORK <u>FINISH</u> */fish/*.

/la-la-la/: far away, long line of people, long list

English	ASL
Our car is parked <u>way over there</u>.	OUR CAR point-far-C <u>/la-la-la/</u>.
I didn't realize there was such a <u>long list</u> of ASL abbreviations.	I NOT REALIZE ASL HAVE ABBREVIATION <u>LONG-LIST</u> <u>/la-la-la/</u>.

/mmm—puckered lips/: medium size, regular, enjoying doing something

English	ASL
The boys want a <u>medium</u> cheese pizza.	BOY WANT CHEESE PIZZA <u>MEDIUM</u> <u>/mmm/</u>.
We had fun yesterday <u>just driving around</u>.	----------TI---------- YESTERDAY WE HAVE FUN <u>DRIVE-AROUND</u> <u>/mmm/</u>.

/oo/: cold, old, small, thin, what to do, who

English	ASL
I'll have a <u>small</u> diet soda, please.	PLEASE, I WANT SODA DIET [fs], <u>SMALL</u> <u>/oo/</u>.
<u>What</u> is that <u>really skinny</u> girl <u>doing</u>?	--------------------T------------------ ---------WQ--------- GIRL <u>THIN /oo/</u> THERE, <u>#DO-DO /oo/</u>?

/pah/: at last, finally

English	ASL
Lynn <u>finally</u> became a teacher of the deaf.	LYNN [fs] <u>FINALLY</u> <u>/pah/</u> BECOME TEACHER FOR DEAF.
Carmy graduated with her interpreting certificate <u>at long last</u>.	<u>AT-LAST</u> <u>/pah/</u>, CARMY [fs] GRADUATE, GET INTERPRETING CERTIFICATE.

/puffed cheeks/: fat, long ago, many (with CL:Bent 55), tired

English	ASL
That dog is <u>really fat</u>.	---------------T-------------- DOG THAT-ONE <u>FAT</u> */puffed cheeks/*.
<u>Once upon a time</u> in a country <u>far away</u>...	LONG-AGO */puffed cheeks/*, COUNTRY FAR */puffed cheeks/*. . .

/so/: close call, cold, curious, delicious, good riddance, hard, tired

English	ASL
I enjoy a <u>cold</u> drink on a hot day.	HOT DAY, I ENJOY <u>COLD</u> */so/* DRINK.
We were surprised that the avocado ice cream was <u>delicious</u>!	SURPRISE US AVOCADO [fs] ICE-CREAM <u>DELICIOUS</u> */so/*!

/th/: awkward, careless, clumsy, don't like, dirty, drunk, lazy, not yet

English	ASL
Pigs are <u>dirty</u>.	--T-- PIG <u>DIRTY</u> */th/*.
Johnnie is an <u>awkward</u> dancer.	--------T------- JOHNNIE [fs] <u>DANCE</u> */th/*.
Drew is lazy and has<u>n't</u> finished <u>yet</u>.	-----T----- -------N------- DREW [fs] <u>LAZY</u> */th/*, FINISH <u>NOT-YET</u> */th/*.

/wah/: don't want, want, what?, why?

English	ASL
Grandma never <u>wants</u> to eat fish.	GRANDMA NEVER <u>WANT</u> */wah/* EAT FISH.
<u>What</u>? <u>Why not</u>?	<u>WHAT</u> */wah/*! <u>WHY-NOT</u> */wah/*?

BEGINNING-INTERMEDIATE LEVEL

/bro/: break/broken, broke (no money), burned-out light bulb

English	ASL
Makenzie broke the chair.	MAKENZIE [fs] BROKE /bro/ CHAIR.
After her Christmas shopping spree, my mother was broke.	CHRISTMAS SHOP++ FINISH, MY MOTHER BROKE /bro/.

/clenched teeth/: emphatic for clean, expensive, hot, large, loud, smart

English	ASL
The blue whale is the largest animal.	-----------T---------- BLUE WHALE LARGEST /clenched teeth/ ANIMAL.
Our ASL teacher is so smart,	----------------T--------------- OUR ASL TEACHER SMART /clenched teeth/.

/closed mouth and long chin/: can, don't mind, maybe, oh I see, possible

English	ASL
Can Leigh fly a plane?	-----T----- --------------------------------Q------------------ PLANE, CAN /closed mouth and long chin/ ----------Q------------------ LEIGH [fs] DRIVE?
Please close the door, if you don't mind.	--------------------------CC------------------------ YOU DON'T-MIND /closed mouth --------CC--------- and long chin/, DOOR-CLOSE, PLEASE.
There's no mail today because it's a federal holiday. Oh, I see.	------TI----- ----N---- ---RQ--- TODAY NONE MAIL, WHY? FEDERAL -------Y------ HOLIDAY. OH-I-SEE /closed mouth and long chin/.

/for-for/: what for?

English	ASL
<u>What</u> are you asking me <u>for</u>?	--------------WQ------------ YOU-ASK-ME <u>WHAT-FOR</u> */for-for/*?
<u>What</u> do you need to know <u>for</u>?	-----------WQ----------- YOU NEED KNOW <u>FOR-FOR</u> */for-for/*?

/off/: break up *(courtship)*, get off, remove, take down, take off

English	ASL
Kindly <u>remove</u> your cap.	PLEASE <u>CAP-OFF</u> */off/*.
Those dirty curtains need to be <u>taken down</u> and washed.	DIRTY CURTAIN THERE-C NEED <u>TAKE-DOWN</u> */off/*, WASH-IN-MACHINE.

/pow/: explode, hit hard, hot temper, repress, shoot a gun

English	ASL
I love to watch <u>fireworks</u> over the ocean on the Fourth of July.	-------TI----- JULY 4th, I KISS-FIST WATCH -----RQ----- <u>FIREWORKS</u> */pow++/* WHERE? OCEAN.
Last night my brother <u>shot</u> three soda cans.	----------TI---------- ---------------T--------------- LAST NIGHT, THREE SODA CAN MY BROTHER <u>PULL-TRIGGER++</u> */pow, pow, pow/*.

/ps-ps/: chic, elegant, fancy, sophisticated

English	ASL
The European castle had <u>elegant</u> furniture.	THERE-R EUROPE CASTLE [fs] HAVE <u>FANCY</u> */ps-ps/* FURNITURE.
Jackie is wearing a <u>formal</u> suit.	JACKIE [fs] WEAR SUIT <u>FORMAL</u> */ps-ps/*.

/pursed lips/: concentrate, persevere, read carefully, stubborn, work hard

English	ASL
Addison <u>worked hard</u> on the album.	ADDISON [fs] <u>WORK</u> */pursed lips/* PICTURE BOOK.
<u>Read</u> that contract <u>carefully</u> before you sign it.	CONTRACT THERE-L, YOU <u>READ</u> */pursed lips/* FINISH, SIGN.

/sow/: so cold, so dirty, so embarrassed, so hard, so tired

English	ASL
Mom and Dad moved out of North Dakota because of the <u>frigid</u> winters.	MOTHER, FATHER MOVE OUT ND --RQ-- WHY? WINTER <u>COLD</u> */sow/*.
Receptive fingerspelling is <u>so hard</u>!	FINGERSPELLING RECEPTIVE <u>HARD</u> */sow/*!

/sta-sta/: long process, struggle

English	ASL
The authors of this book <u>wrote continuously</u> for four years.	----------T---------- THIS BOOK, AUTHOR TWO-OF-THEM <u>WRITE-CONTINUOUSLY</u>*/sta-sta/* FOUR YEAR FINISH.
It's a <u>continual struggle</u> for ASL students to learn mouth morphemes.	------------------------T----------------------- LEARN MOUTH-MORPHEME ASL STUDENT <u>STRUGGLE++</u> */sta-sta/*.

/tongue out and down/: accident, exaggerate, indigestion, lousy, ugh

English	ASL
Grandpa feels <u>tired</u>; he has <u>bad indigestion</u>.	GRANDPA FEEL <u>TIRED</u>; HAVE <u>INDIGESTION</u> */tongue out and down/*.
I'm <u>starving</u>, but this soup is <u>lousy</u>, <u>ugh</u>!	I <u>HUNGRY</u> */tongue out and down/*, BUT SOUP <u>LOUSY, UGH</u> */tongue out and down/*!

/tut/: been to/visited/want to visit, touch

English	ASL
Have you ever <u>been to</u> Israel?	-----T----- --------------------Q------------------- ISRAEL, YOU FINISH <u>TOUCH</u> */tut/*?
We <u>want to visit</u> Paris.	WE WANT <u>TOUCH</u> */tut/* PARIS.
Small children love to <u>touch</u> everything.	CHILDREN-SMALL KISS-FIST EVERYTHING <u>TOUCH</u> */tut++/*.

/wrong/: error, mistake, wrong

English	ASL
The student made four <u>errors</u>.	STUDENT <u>WRONG</u> */wrong/* FOUR.
Marrying that man was a <u>big mistake</u>!	I MARRY MAN THAT-ONE, <u>MISTAKE /wrong/</u>, WOW!

INTERMEDIATE LEVEL

/bounce tongue up and down repeatedly/: hello, later, look (at)

English	ASL
Quick! <u>Look at</u> the duck!	<u>LOOK /wag tongue/</u> DUCK!
<u>Hello</u> everyone!	<u>HELLO++ /wag tongue/</u>!

/bow/: burned-out light, eyes-popped-out/stunning

English	ASL
The kitchen light bulb is <u>burned out</u>. It needs to be replaced.	LIGHT THERE KITCHEN BURN-OUT */bow/*; MUST REPLACE LIGHT.
Dad was <u>stunned</u> at the amount of his Christmas bonus check!	FATHER HE CHRISTMAS BONUS CHECK LOOK-AT, <u>EYE-POP-OUT /bow/</u>!

/fi^^sh (wiggle tongue)/: finish after a long task

English	ASL
Kevin <u>finally finished</u> writing his book.	KEVIN [fs] PAH <u>FINISH</u> /fi^^sh/ WRITE HIS BOOK.
After 11 months of research, Ginger <u>finally finished</u> her doctoral dissertation.	AFTER 11 MONTH RESEARCH, GINGER [fs] HER DISSERTATION <u>FINISH</u> /fi^^sh/.

/fus/: PhD

English	ASL
Gallaudet University offers a few <u>PhD</u> programs.	GALLAUDET OFFER FEW <u>PHD</u> /fus/ PROGRAM.
Most <u>PhD</u> students are in their 30s.	MOST <u>PHD</u> /fus/ STUDENT OLD 30s.

/lick once/: run out, swallow, tired of

English	ASL
I'm sorry that the popcorn is <u>all gone</u>.	I SORRY POPCORN <u>RUN-OUT</u> /lick/.
Don<u>'t</u> argue with me <u>anymore</u>.	--------------------T------------------ YOU ARGUE-WITH-ME, I <u>TIRED-OF</u> /lick/.

/ma-ma-ma/: obsession with money

English	ASL
It serves no purpose in life if one <u>lives solely for money</u>.	------------------------------CC----------------------------- IF <u>MONEY++</u> /ma-ma-ma/ EVERYDAY, LIFE #NG+.
<u>Dwelling on money</u> problems is not good for one's mental health.	NOT GOOD FOR MIND HEALTH <u>THINK-CONTINUALLY</u> /ma-ma-ma/ <u>MONEY</u> PROBLEM.

/pensive/: expensive

English	ASL
A Jaguar is <u>expensive</u>.	CAR JAGUAR [fs] <u>EXPENSIVE</u> /pensive/.
It's <u>expensive</u> to live in Honolulu.	LIVE HONOLULU <u>EXPENSIVE</u> /pensive/.

/po/: competent, good at, knowledgeable, notice/see/spot, shot-H (better than/more than), zap

English	ASL
Einstein was <u>knowledgeable about</u> mathematics.	EINSTEIN [fs] BEFORE <u>KNOWLEDGE-ABLE</u> /po/ MATH.
William Hoy was an <u>outstanding</u> pro baseball outfielder. <u>/po/</u>	PRO [fs] BASEBALL THERE [ix R], MAN NAME WILLIAM [fs] HOY [fs] <u>GOOD-AT</u> OUTFIELDER [fs].
The shepherd <u>spotted</u> a wolf in the field.	SHEPHERD <u>SPOT</u> /po/ WOLF THERE [ix C] FIELD.
Lai <u>beat</u> Kai at chess.	LAI [fs] [ix R] <u>shot H [ix L]</u> /po/ KAI [fs] FOR CHESS [fs].

/ps/: lucky

English	ASL
You are <u>lucky</u> not to have had a flat tire for the past ten years.	YOU <u>LUCKY</u> /ps/ YOUR CAR NO FLAT-TIRE TEN YEAR SINCE.
That <u>lucky</u> woman just won a decoder as a door prize.	---RQ--- WOMAN THERE-L <u>LUCKY</u> /ps/, WHY? SHE WIN FOR DOOR-PRIZE [fs] CLOSED-CAPTION.

/shh/: gobble, make out, taunt, use exceedingly, wild time

English	ASL

Don't <u>use</u> your sister's phone <u>too often</u>.	`-------------------------------------T-----------------------------`
	<u>USE</u> /shh/ OFTEN YOUR SISTER PHONE
	`-----N-----`
	DON'T.

My dog <u>gobbles up</u> his dinner in about a minute!	`---------------Y-------------` MY DOG DINNER, HE <u>GOBBLE</u> /shh/ 1-MINUTE!

/so/: close call, cold, curious, hard, embarrassed, tired

English	ASL
I was <u>tired</u> after doing yard work.	YARD WORK FINISH, ME <u>TIRED</u> /so/.
The banquet speaker was <u>embarrassed</u> because his fly was down.	FOOD++ LECTURER <u>EMBARRASSED</u> /so/, `---RQ---` WHY? ZIPPER-DOWN.

/wag tongue right and left repeatedly/: feel good, must, really want

English	ASL
Ali <u>really wants</u> to have a mountain cabin.	ALI [fs] <u>REALLY WANT</u> /wag tongue/ HAVE MOUNTAIN CABIN [fs].
My back <u>feels really good</u>! Keep massaging.	MY BACK <u>FEEL GOOD</u> /wag tongue/! CONTINUE MASSAGE.

ADVANCED LEVEL

/ahh (open mouth)/: desperately look for, expression of shock, travel extensively

English	ASL
It takes about five days <u>to drive from</u> San Diego <u>to</u> Washington, DC.	SD-L, WASHINGTON, DC-R, <u>DRIVE L-to-R</u> /ahh/ ABOUT FIVE-DAY.

My two friends were <u>shocked</u> to have twin boys.	MY FRIEND TWO-OF-THEM <u>SHOCK</u> /ahh/ BORN BOY TWIN.

/lm/: expert, proficient, skillful

English	ASL
Dr. David Peikoff was a <u>skillful</u> orator.	MAN NAME DR DAVID [fs] LAST PEIKOFF [fs] HIMSELF <u>SKILLFUL</u> /lm/ SPEAKER.
Engineers must be <u>proficient</u> in math.	ENGINEER <u>PROFICIENT</u> /lm/ MATH MUST.

/uch/: jumbo, large amount

English	ASL
Lu found <u>that large stack</u> of old coins in the sand.	LU [fs] FOUND <u>STACK</u> /luch/ OLD COIN IN SAND.
That little girl has <u>a huge pile</u> of M&Ms.	SMALL GIRL THERE-C HAVE <u>JUMBO-PILE</u> /luch/ MM CANDY.

/m^^s (tongue bounce)/: must

English	ASL
For good health, one <u>must</u> eat plenty of fruits and vegetables every day.	FOR GOOD HEALTH, EVERYDAY PERSON <u>MUST</u> /m^^s/ EAT FRUIT, VEGETABLE PLENTY.

/mum-mum/: nab one by one, win all the games

English	ASL
It is rare for a team to <u>win all the games</u> in the World Series.	TEAM <u>WIN</u> ++ /mum-mum/ ALL GAME IN WORLD SERIES [fs] RARE [fs].

During a successful secret credit card fraud scheme, the cops <u>made many arrests</u>.	SECRET PLAN SUCCEED; COP <u>NAB-MANY-SUSPECT</u> /mum-mum/ RELATE CREDIT-CARD FRAUD [fs].

/po-po/: cannon, car race, speed boat

English	ASL
There is an annual <u>dirt vehicle race</u> in Baja California.	BC HAVE ANNUAL DIRT <u>CAR RACE</u> CL:3 /po-po/.
<u>Driving a speed boat</u> requires skill.	<u>SPEED BOAT</u> CL:B /po-po/ REQUIRE SKILL.

/pow-oo/: boom, forget, stricken

English	ASL
I <u>forgot</u> to pick up the mail.	I <u>FORGOT</u> /pow-oo/ GET MAIL.
My niece was <u>stricken</u> with the flu two days ago.	DAY-BEFORE-YESTERDAY, MY NIECE <u>SICK</u> /pow-oo/ FLU [fs].

/pth/: melt, smash on floor

English	ASL
You see, butter <u>melts</u> fast in hot water.	UNDERSTAND, BUTTER <u>MELT</u> /pth/ FAST IN HOT WATER.
My glasses are on the floor; don't <u>step on them</u>.	MY GLASSES ON FLOOR; NOT <u>SMASH</u> /pth/.

/puckered lips with1-handed "awful" sign/: can't believe it, interesting, wow

English	ASL
<u>Oh, my gosh</u>, look how the boy has grown!	<u>WOW</u> /puckered lips with "awful" sign/! HE (point-boy) GROW-UP-BIG!

| Geez! My father got three tickets today! | YIKES /puckered lips with "awful" sign/! TODAY FATHER GOT THREE DRIVE TICKET! |

/puh/: give in, not again, tendency, willing (*after initial hesitancy*)

English	ASL
Aunt Emma tends to stay home at night.	AUNT EMMA [fs] TEND /puh/ STAY HOME EVERY-NIGHT.
I'm willing to work one more hour.	I WILLING /puh/ WORK 1-MORE HOUR.
A good mother does not give in to a child's tantrum.	----------------N---------------- GOOD MOTHER GIVE-IN /puh/ NONE FOR CHILD TANTRUM.

/pursed lips and twinged nose/: always that way, characteristic, the way it is

English	ASL
Cousin Bess likes to start each new day with the local paper. That's how she is.	COUSIN BESS [fs] LIKE START NEW DAY READ NEWSPAPER. HERS /pursed lips and twinged nose/.
In the old days, it was typical for a car to have an all-metal body.	LONG-AGO, CAR BODY ALL METAL ITS /pursed lips and twinged nose/.

/sweep inside cheek with tongue/: experienced, skilled

English	ASL
The secretary is experienced in fixing the copier.	SECRETARY EXPERIENCED /sweep inside cheek with tongue/ FIX COPY MACHINE.
NBA referees are highly skilled.	NBA REFEREE SKILLED /sweep inside cheek with tongue/.

128

/trilled lips/: engine/helicopter noise, lawn mower, toy car, too good/too much

English	ASL
The Harley Davidson motorcycle engine <u>runs very loudly</u>.	HD MOTORCYCLE ENGINE LOUD <u>RUN</u> <u>/trilled lips/</u>.
Leyton just got a <u>fabulous</u> new job. with a <u>huge pay raise.</u>	LEYTON [fs] NEW JOB <u>VERY-GOOD</u> <u>/trilled lips/</u>, INCOME <u>VERY-GOOD</u> <u>/trilled lips/</u>.

SECTION FIVE:
STUDY QUESTIONS

BEGINNING LEVEL STUDY QUESTIONS
Part A

1. What is the proper facial expression for Wh- questions (who, what, where, etc.)?

   a)

   b)

2. List three possible word orders for Wh- questions in ASL: Who is the teacher?

   a)

   b)

   c)

3. Why do the Wh- question word orders vary?

   a)

   b)

   c)

4. What is the required facial expression for Yes/No questions?

   a)

   b)

5. Write three ways to place a subject pronoun in a sentence in ASL: He is smart.

   a)

   b)

c)

6. What facial grammar do you employ when you affirm a fact?

7. What kinds of changes do you make on the face for negation?

a)

b)

8. List any five directional verbs.

a)

b)

c)

d)

e)

9. List any five non-directional verbs.

a)

b)

c)

d)

e)

10. Explain the purpose for topic marker/topicalization.

11. What facial grammar is required for expressing topicalization?

a)

b)

12. How do you distinguish a noun from a verb in ASL?

Noun: a)   b)

Verb: a)   b)

13. What are suitable substitutions for "very"?

a)

b)

c)

14. Discuss the placement of NOT in the sentence: "It is _not_ good." List three options.

a)

b)

c)

15. List any five modal auxiliary verbs.

a)

b)

c)

d)

e)

16. Write three possible sentence patterns for modals: I need to study math.

a)

b)

c)

BEGINNING LEVEL STUDY QUESTIONS
Part B

1. List the key introductory words for conditional clauses.

    a)

    b)

    c)

    d)

    e)

2. What are the rules for conditional clauses in ASL?

3. What is the appropriate facial grammar for a conditional clause?

    a)

    b)

4. Apart from other uses, what is the purpose for the FINISH conjunction?

5. What is the ASL translation for the idiomatic English phrase "There is/are"?

6. In what two situations does ASL keep the apostrophe /-'s/?

a)

b)

7. How can the apostrophe /-'s/ be replaced?

a)

b)

c)

8. List four purposes for the sign BORED.

a)

b)

c)

d)

9. Make a list of quantifiers for count nouns and non-count nouns:

Count Nouns	Non-Count Nouns
a)	a)
b)	b)
c)	c)

10. Where do you place a quantifier in a sentence?

a)

b)

c)

11. What is the ASL assumption for singularity and plurality?

12. Each of these three pronoun categories is characterized by which handshape?

a) Personal Pronouns

b) Possessive Pronouns

c) Reflexive Pronouns

BEGINNING-INTERMEDIATE LEVEL STUDY QUESTIONS
Part A

1. What roles does a classifier provide?

   a)

   b)

   c)

   d)

   e)

2. Explain the purpose for each role above.

   a)

   b)

   c)

   d)

   e)

3. Where are time concepts placed in a sentence? Why?

4. Discuss the placement of ASL adjectives.

5. When is an adjective placed after a noun? Why?

6. What are frequency words?

7. Where are frequency words placed?

8. Why does frequency placement differ from time concept placement?

9. How many lexical-based signs, or fingerspelled loan signs, are there?

10. List five examples of loan signs:

a)

b)

c)

d)

e)

11. List any five mouth morphemes and explain their purposes:

a)   a)

b)   b)

c)   c)

d)   d)

e)   e)

12. List any five negative signs:

a)

b)

c)

d)

e)

BEGINNING-INTERMEDIATE LEVEL STUDY QUESTIONS
Part B

1. What is the difference between repeated and continuous elements?

   Repeated element:

   Continuous element:

2. How is plurality expressed in ASL without numbers or quantifiers?

   a)

   b)

   c)

   d)

   e)

3. How is "very" replaced in ASL?

   a)

   b)

   c)

4. List three professions that require the use of the agent suffix and three that do not require the suffix.

   Job with Agent Suffix:

   a)

   b)

   c)

<u>Job without Agent Suffix</u>:

a)

b)

c)

5. What is a rhetorical question (RQ)?

6. What facial grammar is necessary for rhetorical questions?

a)

b)

7. Where in the sentence are the proper places for a rhetorical question?

8. In general, how long does one wait before using a rhetorical question again?

9. Apart from English, what is unusual about the use of WORSE in ASL?

10. In what situations can you reverse the palm orientation (from front to back) for numbers 6 to 9?

a)

b)

11. For reinforcement, enumerate/list the purposes for classifiers:

a)

b)

c)

d)

e)

12. While in English only nouns and verbs have plurality, which parts of speech in ASL can be pluralized?

a)

b)

c)

INTERMEDIATE LEVEL STUDY QUESTIONS
Part A

1. How does one address a deaf person?

2. How many ways are there in ASL to pluralize nouns?

3. List the seven methods of pluralization:

    a)

    b)

    c)

    d)

    e)

    f)

    g)

4. Which is preferred?

5. What is the general rule for ASL adjective placement?

6. What is the rule for when not to mouth?

7. What do you know about ASL infinitives?

8. When does ASL use DID?

9. Memorize all (approximately 20) past tense verbs that are permitted in ASL.

10. What are the exceptions for pluralization (using the ending /-s/)?

11. For the possessive case of nouns, when does ASL keep the apostrophe?

12. For reflexive pronouns, read ASL Notes 1 and 2; note adding intensity for commands.

13. When do some signed adjectives move once?

14. Which articles does ASL keep and which are deleted?

15. What are the rules for using the comparative form of adjectives?

   a)

   b)

   c)

   d)

16. How are reflexive pronouns used as verbs?

17. What are five kinds of auxiliary ASL verbs?

   a)

   b)

   c)

   d)

   e)

18. Give examples for directional, partial-directional and non-directional ASL verbs:

Directional	Partial-directional	Non-directional
a)	a)	a)
b)	b)	b)
c)	c)	c)

d)   d)   d)

e)   e)   e)

19. What are the roles of active voice and passive voice in both English and ASL?

20. How are they used in ASL?

INTERMEDIATE LEVEL STUDY QUESTIONS
Part B

1. What is the fundamental difference between WON'T and REFUSE in ASL?

2. List any two negative prefixes.

   a)

   b)

3. Where are frequency adverbs placed in the ASL sentence: "I <u>often</u> go bowling"?

   a)

   b)

   c)

   d)

4. What are two things one must do for time indicator?

   a)

   b)

5. Explain preposition changes for day, week, month and year.

   a) Day:

   b) Week:

   c) Month:

   d) Year:

6. Give two examples of prepositions that are replaced or deleted in ASL.

a)

b)

7. For what primary purposes are prepositions used in ASL?

8. What are four coordinating conjunctions?

a)

b)

c)

d)

9. What are five substitutions for "and"?

a)

b)

c)

d)

e)

10. What are the four correlative conjunctions in English and their ASL counterparts?

English	ASL
a)	a)
b)	b)

148

    c)   c)

    d)   d)

11. How are interjections expressed in ASL?

    a)

    b)

    c)

12. How is "there is/ there are" indicated in ASL?

13. What are two things you must do to indicate a topic marker?

    a)

    b)

14. How do you determine the difference between Q and WQ?

    Q:

    WQ:

15. Write an example sentence for a Yes/No question in both English and ASL.

    English:

    ASL:

16. What is a rhetorical question [RQ]?

17. Write an example sentence for a Wh- question and one for a rhetorical question.

WQ:

RQ:

18. Write two example sentences incorporating different conditional clauses:

a)

b)

19. What is the rule for fingerspelling the year?

20. Write the names of the twelve months as fingerspelled:

a)

b)

c)

d)

e)

f)

g)

h)

i)

j)

k)

l)

21. Write any four examples of FS loan signs:

a)

b)

c)

d)

22. Memorize all idiomatic expressions listed for both ASL and English in the first six pages.

23. Memorize all mouth morphemes listed up to and including the Intermediate Level.

ADVANCED LEVEL STUDY QUESTIONS
Part A

1. Which part(s) of speech, in both ASL and English, have ending markers/suffixes?

English | ASL

a)   a)

b)   b)

c)   c)

d)   d)

2. What are English verb types that don't exist in ASL?

a)

b)

c)

3. When can you put time concepts towards the end of a sentence?

4. Write two ASL examples where "and" is not expressed in names or phrases.

a)

b)

5. What are four differences between English and ASL correlative conjunctions?

English | ASL

a)   a)

b)   b)

c)   c)

d)   d)

6. When are prepositions generally used in ASL?

7. How can Wh- questions become Yes/No questions?

a)

b)

c)

d)

8. How do ASL tag questions differ from English tag questions?

a)

b)

c)

9. When is an ASL adverb clause put at the end of a sentence?

10. When does one fingerspell in a circle?

a)

b)

11. Which words go with the fingerspelled IT?

    a)

    b)

    c)

    d)

    e)

    f)

    g)

12. What are some phrases where IT not is expressed in ASL?

    a)

    b)

13. What are the corresponding ASL translations of English prefixes?

    a)

    b)

    c)

    d)

    e)

    f)

    g)

14. Under what circumstances are the numbers 1-5 displayed up front?

a)

b)

c)

d)

e)

f)

15. How does one recognize a fingerspelled loan sign, as distinguished from regular fingerspelling?

a)

b)

c)

d)

16. How often is a rhetorical question signed?

ADVANCED LEVEL STUDY QUESTIONS
Part B

1. List any five intensifiers:

a)

b)

c)

d)

e)

2. What are Wh-words used without facial expression called?

3. List three types of verbs; write a sentence with an example of each:

a)

b)

c)

4. What is one exception for using the verb "To Be" in ASL?

5. If there are several time concepts within a sentence, how does one determine the word order?

6. Explain the difference in ASL ~ English usage for "of," "in," "on" and "off."

7. List five verbs that use head-nodding for affirmation:

a)

b)

c)

d)

e)

8. List five Wh-words that also have a fingerspelled form, but only for WQ purposes, and that are used in isolation:

a)

b)

c)

d)

e)

9. For what four purposes are these Wh-words fingerspelled?

a)

b)

c)

d)

10. Which two adverbial clauses are questionable for their use in ASL?

a)

b)

11. For reinforcement purposes, list five uses for classifiers:

a)

b)

c)

d)

e)

12. ASL does not use "AND" with which part of speech—nouns, adjectives or verbs?

13. "WILL" for future tense does not always need to be signed. When does it <u>not</u> need to be signed?

14. What are three ways to translate the English word "of" into ASL?

a)

b)

c)

15. What are the key ASL words for one type of linking verb: sensory verbs?

16. The Rule of 9 can be used with seconds, minutes, hours, days, weeks, years, cents, dollars and age. With which of these can the number 10 be used?

a)

b)

c)

17. List the names of the months that must be abbreviated in fingerspelling:

a)

b)

c)

d)

e)

f)

g)

18. What are the three reasons for a signer to use a double pronoun?

a)

b)

c)

19. "ONCE" has two meanings. One is for time. How is the other meaning signed?

20. /cha/ is the mouth morpheme for large size, height and length. What is mouthed for something bigger, taller or longer?

KEY FOR BEGINNING LEVEL STUDY QUESTIONS
Part A

1. The proper facial expressions for Wh- questions are:

   a) scrunched eyebrows

   b) head tilted forward or sideways

2. Three different word order patterns for Wh- questions:

   English: <u>Who</u> is the teacher?

             -----------WQ------------
   ASL: a) <u>WHO</u> TEACHER? (Keep facial expression to the end of the question.)

                  ---WQ---
          b) TEACHER <u>WHO</u>? (Save facial expression for the end of the question.)

             -----------------WQ------------------
          c) <u>WHO</u> TEACHER <u>WHO</u>? (Use double interrogative pronoun for emphasis.)

3. The reasons for varying word order for Wh- questions are:

   a) first for short questions

   b) second for long questions

   c) third for emphasis

   (<u>Note</u>: See examples in 2, above.)

4. The proper facial expression for Yes/No questions are:

   a) raised eyebrows

   b) head tilted forward or sideways

5. The placement options for subject pronouns in ASL include:

   a) <u>HE</u> SMART.

b) SMART <u>HE</u>.

c) <u>HE</u> SMART <u>HE</u>. (for emphasis)

6. Nod head to show affirmation.

7. For negation, squeeze eyebrows and shake head.

8. There are about 25 full directional verbs in ASL, including:

   a) ASK

   b) HELP

   c) MOVE

   c) PAY

   d) SHOW

9. Here are a few examples of non-directional verbs:

   a) EAT

   b) SMELL

   c) STUDY

   d) THINK

   e) WANT

10. For topicalization, place the main idea up front, to be followed with supporting details. That way listeners know what is being talked about quickly. This is a common sentence structure, but don't overuse it.

11. For proper non-manual behaviors accompanying topicalization, raise eyebrows for the first part of the sentence, then drop brows for the rest of the sentence. The --T-- tends to be a single word or two words long, but can be several:

```
-----------T------------
```
<u>DISNEYLAND</u> POPULAR VACATION PLACE.

```
-------------------------------------------T-----------------------------------------
```
<u>WHITE CAT THERE FIRE DEPARTMENT BUILDING</u> NAME VANILLA [fs].

12. <u>Verbs</u> are characterized by a single movement and a bigger signing space; <u>nouns</u> are identified by multiple movements and a smaller signing space.

<u>Examples</u>: OPEN-DOOR   DOOR

           SIT   CHAIR

           EAT   FOOD

           GROW   PLANT

13. Suitable substitutions for "very":

    a) WOW

    b) REAL/REALLY

    c) increased intensity with facial expression and increased speed in signing

14. Three ways to place NOT:

```
   ---N---
```
    a) <u>NOT</u> GOOD

```
          ---N---
```
    b) GOOD <u>NOT</u>

```
   ----------------N--------------
```
    c) <u>NOT</u> GOOD <u>NOT</u>   (for emphasis)

162

15. <u>Modal auxiliary verbs</u>:

    a) CAN

    b) CAN'T

    c) HAVE-TO

    d) MAY

    e) MUST

    f) NEED

    g) OUGHT-TO

    h) SHOULD

16. <u>English</u>: I <u>need</u> to study math.

    <u>ASL</u>: a) I <u>NEED</u> STUDY MATH. (<u>Note</u>: Delete "to.")

        b) I STUDY MATH <u>NEED</u>.

        c) I <u>NEED</u> STUDY MATH <u>NEED</u>.

KEY FOR BEGINNING LEVEL STUDY QUESTIONS
Part B

1. Key signed words for CC: AFTER, BEFORE, IF/SUPPOSE, SINCE, WHEN/HAPPEN:

    ------------------CC---------------
    AFTER GAME FINISH, WE GO RESTAURANT.

    -----------------------CC---------------------
    BEFORE WE WATCH MOVIE, WE EAT OUT.

    ------------------CC--------------
    IF YOU COME EARLY, I CAN TELL YOU NEWS.

    -------------------------CC---------------------
    WHEN/HAPPEN YOU ARRIVE, PLEASE WAIT.

2. CC Rules: Place the CC phrase up front in an ASL sentence. (This happens about 95% of the time.) The CC in an English sentence can come either before or after the main clause. The CC in any sentence is a dependent adverbial clause modifying the verb in the main clause. The main clause can stand alone, but the CC cannot.

3. Proper facial expression for CC:

    a) raise eyebrows

    b) sometimes (but not required) tilt head backward a bit

4. The FINISH conjunction serves as "then."

    English: I ate breakfast, then went to work and finally to school.

    ASL: I EAT BREAKFAST FINISH, GO WORK FINISH, GO SCHOOL.

5. The idiomatic English "there is"/"there are"; "there was"/"there were" are signed HAVE in ASL. (ASL does not use HAS or HAD.)

Also, the adverbial object of the preposition from the English sentence becomes the subject of the ASL sentence.

English: <u>There is</u> a squirrel on <u>the picnic table</u>.

ASL: <u>PICNIC TABLE</u> <u>HAVE</u> SQUIRREL.

English: <u>There are</u> many ideas in <u>the program</u>.

ASL: <u>PROGRAM</u> <u>HAVE</u> MANY IDEA.

6. There are two situations for using an apostrophe:

    a) Proper nouns; proper names = Applebee<u>'s</u>, Lowe<u>'s</u>, Trader Joe<u>'s</u>; Lou<u>'s</u> condo

    b) Possession = My uncle<u>'s</u> 1956 Bel Air car

(<u>Note</u>: Do <u>not</u> put an apostrophe for a decade <u>plural</u>, 1970<u>'s</u>. The proper English is 1970<u>s</u> or '70<u>s</u>.)

7. The English possessive /-'s/

    a) can be kept in ASL: KENDALL<u>'S</u>

    b) can be replaced with a possessive pronoun: KENDALL <u>HIS</u>

    c) can be left out altogether: KENDALL /Ø/

English: Kendall<u>'s</u> surfboard is in the garage.

<u>ASL a)</u> KENDALL<u>'S</u> SURFBOARD IN GARAGE.

<u>ASL b)</u> KENDALL [fs] <u>HIS</u> SURFBOARD IN GARAGE.

<u>ASL c)</u> KENDALL [fs] SURFBOARD IN GARAGE.

8. Three purposes for "bored" in English:

    a) Lack of activity: I am <u>bored</u> tonight.

    b) Lack of interest: This movie <u>bores</u> me.

    c) Make a hole: The plumber <u>bored</u> two holes in the wall.

ASL has all the above plus one more purpose:

d) Not wanting to do a particular activity (<u>Note</u>: This is considered strong ASL.)

<u>English</u>: I don't want to go to Vons today.

<u>ASL</u>: TODAY I <u>BORED</u> GO VONS [fs].

9. | <u>Count Nouns</u> | <u>Non-count Nouns</u> |
    | --- | --- |
    | a) cent, dollar | a) money |
    | b) game, sport | b) tennis, golf, swimming |
    | c) pie crust | c) flour, butter, salt, shortening |

10. What is a quantifier? It tells how many nouns there are: "few," "many," "none," "several," "some" or a specific number. In ASL, you can place a quantifier before a noun, following a noun or both:

a) <u>FEW</u> CAT

b) CAT <u>FEW</u>

c) <u>FEW</u> CAT <u>FEW</u> (for emphasis)

11. English users love <u>plurality</u>; ASL users love <u>singularity</u>. Consequently, ASL uses singular signs when it means plural. (Native signers rely on life experiences to decide on singularity or plurality.)

<u>English</u>: I love dog<u>s</u>.

<u>ASL</u>: I LOVE <u>DOG</u>.

<u>English</u>: Please bring paper plate<u>s</u> to the party.

<u>ASL</u>: PLEASE BRING PAPER <u>PLATE</u> PARTY.
(<u>Note</u>: Who would bring only one plate?)

12. Specific handshapes for pronouns:

<u>Personal</u> pronouns (I, YOU, HE/SHE/IT, WE, THEY) = index finger

<u>Possessive</u> pronouns (MY/MINE, YOUR/YOURS, HIS/HERS/ITS, OUR/OURS, YOUR/YOURS) = open B palm

<u>Reflexive</u> pronouns (MYSELF, YOURSELF, HIMSELF, HERSELF, ITSELF, OURSELVES, YOURSELVES) = A or Open A, PO center; MM /sef/ (= mouth morpheme for reflexive pronouns)

KEY FOR BEGINNING-INTERMEDIATE LEVEL
STUDY QUESTIONS
Part A

1. Classifiers help provide specific information in the following areas:

   a) Location

   b) Movement

   c) Description

   d) Pluralization

   e) Orientation

2. Classifier purposes include:

   a) Location (far, near, left, right, front, back, up, down, etc.)

   b) Movement (speed, direction, stationary, straight, zigzag, etc.)

   c) Description (shape, texture and size)

   d) Pluralization (how many and how much)

   e) Orientation (set up)

3. ASL has a tendency to set up a tense indicator at the beginning to establish the tense up front. It is for one specific time concept, not for frequency. Unlike English, the tense does not have to be repeated with every verb in the conversation.

4. ASL is more flexible than English for placing an adjective in a sentence.

5. Adjectives would need to be placed after a noun if there are more than two adjectives to avoid memory overload.

6. Frequency words include: "always," "never," "once," "sometimes," "every week," "every other year," etc.

7. Frequency words can be placed anywhere in a sentence.

8. Frequency words are more flexible than one specific time concept, such as "tomorrow," "last month," "this morning," etc.

9. There are more than 85 fingerspelled loan signs.

10. Randomly selected loan sign examples include:

   a) #BANK

   b) #BUSY

   c) #CAR

   d) #EARLY

11. Randomly selected mouth morphemes:

   a) /Cha/ is for conveying large size, tall height, long length.

   b) /Pah/ is intended for "finally" (not for "succeed").

   c) /Puffed cheeks/ illustrate overweight or exhaustion.

   d) /Oo/ has different possibilities, like old, thin, pretty, small, who, etc.

12. Negative signs include:

   a) NOT/DON'T

   b) NEVER

   c) DON'T-WANT/DON'T-LIKE/DON'T-KNOW

   d) WON'T/REFUSE

   e) NO/#NO

   f) NONE/NOTHING

KEY FOR BEGINNING-INTERMEDIATE LEVEL
STUDY QUESTIONS
Part B

1. <u>Repeated action</u> and <u>continuous action</u> differ from each other by movement. The continuous factor happens more often than the repeated factor: For repeated action, move back and forth or pause briefly between actions; for continuous action, move non-stop in a circular motion.

2. <u>Plurality</u> without numbers or quantifiers is signified by:

   a) Reduplication/repetition. Use /++/ symbol: TREE++, BOOK++

   b) Classifiers: CL:1, CL:3, CL:A, CL:B, CL:C, etc.

   c) Cluster affixes (TEAM, CLASS, GROUP/CATEGORY, FAMILY)

   d) Demonstrative pronouns (THESE/THOSE)

   e) Plural pronouns (WE, YOU-PLURAL, THEY)

3. There is no sign for "very" in ASL. Replace "very" with:

   a) REAL/REALLY

   b) WOW

   c) added intensity to both the signing and the facial expression:

   English: "<u>Very</u> hot"

   ASL:

   a) <u>HOT</u>! (bold movement and facial expression)

   b) <u>REAL</u> HOT

   c) <u>WOW</u> HOT

4. Any three professions <u>with agent suffix</u>:

   a) TEACHER

b) LAWYER

c) PREACHER

Any three professions <u>without agent suffix</u>:

a) PRESIDENT

b) DOCTOR

c) COP

5. A rhetorical question is a sentence type that involves a question followed immediately by an answer. The symbol RQ is required labeling in gloss. The RQ happens more often in ASL than in English, but don't overdo it.

6. The RQ facial expression is characterized by raised eyebrows and forward head. The majority of the time, the RQ is used with the Wh- question words.

    <u>English</u>: I cannot make it to class <u>due to</u> a dead battery.

        ----N----   ---RQ---
    <u>ASL</u>: I CAN'T GO CLASS, <u>WHY</u>? BATTERY SHUT-DOWN.

7. The RQ normally occurs in the middle of the sentence; it can also happen at the beginning, but NEVER at the end. Why not? In this case, you would leave out the requisite answer.

8. How often is it acceptable for an RQ to be used? There is no hard rule, but by tradition, the normal frequency would be every 20-50 sentences. In truth, some rarely use it, while others use it all the time, same as in English.

9. What is strange about the sign "worse" used in ASL? It is strange that ASL uses "worse" for something better, more, greater, etc.

    <u>English</u>: I have <u>more books than you</u>.

    <u>ASL</u>: BOOK MINE <u>WORSE THAN</u> YOURS.

In actuality, this idiomatic element "worse" is used mostly among adolescents and young adult signers.

10. You know the rules for displaying numbers with palm orientation [PO] forward or inward. There is an exception for the numbers between 1 and 9 where the numbers are signed with PO inward—height: 1'8", 2'5", 3'7", 4'9", 5'2", 6'6", 6'11", 7'4", etc.

11. The purposes for <u>classifiers</u> include:

   a) Show location

   b) Delineate how many and how much

   c) Show shape and size

   d) Indicate movement (speed, direction)

   e) Illustrate orientation (set-up)

12. In English, the suffix /-s/ is added to most nouns to indicate plurality and to the third person singular, present tense verb to indicate singularity.

<u>English examples of /-s/</u>:

   a) I have cat<u>s</u> (plural noun).

   b) She swim<u>s</u> daily (present tense singular verb, indicating one girl).

In ASL, to what parts of speech can the suffix /-s/, or other suffixes, be added for pluralization?

   a) <u>Nouns</u>: only a few involving fingerspelling, such as MILE<u>S</u>, BILL<u>S</u>, HOUR<u>S</u>

   b) <u>Adjectives</u>: DIFFERENT++ COLOR; BLUE++ BOX

   c) <u>Verbs</u>: MEET++ OLD FRIEND; ORDER++ BOOK

<u>Examples</u>:

   <u>English</u>: Shelby has <u>many</u> different plant<u>s</u>.

   <u>ASL</u>: SHELBY [fs] HAVE PLANT DIFFERENT<u>++</u>.

English: Mother sends <u>lots of</u> Christmas card<u>s</u>.

ASL: CHRISTMAS CARD MOTHER SEND<u>++</u>.

English: The student<u>s</u> gave me their homework.

ASL: STUDENT FINISH <u>GIVE-ME++</u> HOMEWORK.

KEY FOR INTERMEDIATE LEVEL STUDY QUESTIONS
Part A

1. Address a deaf person by waving a hand, tapping the shoulder, stomping the table or floor, etc. It is hearing behavior to call someone's name.

2. There are seven methods for pluralizing nouns.

3. The seven methods include:

a) Use a number, if known.

b) Use a quantifier (FEW, MANY, SOME, etc.).

c) Use a cluster affix (CLASS, GROUP, TEAM, etc.).

d) Use a plural demonstrative pronoun (THESE, THOSE).

e) Use reduplication/repetition (++).

f) Use a plural pronoun (WE, YOU-PLURAL, THEY).

g) Use a classifier.

4. The most preferred pluralization method is numbers: <u>FIVE</u> CAR, <u>TEN</u> YEAR. Why? Numbers are clear and specific. <u>Note</u>: Deaf people love numbers.

5. There are four places to put an adjective in an ASL sentence:

a) Before a noun: <u>HOT</u> DAY

b) After a noun: DAY <u>HOT</u>

c) Both before and after a noun for emphasis: <u>HOT</u> DAY <u>HOT</u>

d) If there are <u>more than two</u> adjectives, always place them <u>after</u> the noun:

   <u>LONG</u> <u>HOT</u> WEEKEND = OK, because only two adjectives.

   <u>old</u>, <u>soft</u>, <u>red</u> ball = OK for English, but not for ASL.

---T---
     BALL <u>OLD</u>, <u>SOFT</u>, <u>RED</u> = perfect ASL, why? To avoid memory overload, it is easier to know and remember the topic if it is placed before a long description.

6. Do not mouth the second subject pronoun when it is repeated at the end of the sentence:

   HE SMART <u>HE</u>. (Don't mouth the last HE.)

Also, don't mouth <u>subject</u> pronouns when they occur after the verb:

   SICK <u>I</u>. (Don't mouth this <u>subject</u> pronoun when it appears at the end.)

It is acceptable to mouth <u>direct object</u> pronouns: ME, YOU, HIM, HER, US, THEM.

<u>Example</u>: MY MOTHER KNOW <u>HIM</u>, <u>HER</u>, <u>THEM</u>, <u>US</u>.

7. There are no infinitive verb forms in ASL. English infinitives have a "to" marker to indicate the unconjugated, or base, form of the verb: <u>to</u> eat, <u>to</u> sleep, <u>to</u> study.

   <u>English</u>: I want <u>to succeed</u> in ASL III.

   <u>ASL</u>: I WANT <u>SUCCEED</u> ASL III.

8. ASL uses DID for a specific circumstance, namely to defend one's position:

   I <u>DID</u> [fs] PAY FOR CLASS. (DID is fingerspelled, not signed.)

9. There is a box listing special verbs with modified spelling for past tense in the *Handbook*. Memorize all—approximately twenty modified verbs.

10. Related to Questions #2, #3 and #4, see the seven methods in the *Handbook*. ASL does use the plural ending marker /–s/ for pluralizations like BILL<u>S</u> or MILE<u>S</u>. Also, MANY CHILD++, TEN PARENT++; these are ASL exceptions.

11. The apostrophe is sometimes deleted, like MOTHER DAY, LION CLUB. For proper nouns, ASL keeps the restaurant or store names that are spelled with an apostrophe: Coco<u>'s</u>, Denny<u>'s</u>, Lowe<u>'s</u>, Macy<u>'s</u>, Trader Joe<u>'s</u>, etc. The apostrophe can also be used to show possession in three different ways:

a) MY MOTHER'S CAR

b) MY MOTHER HER CAR

c) MY MOTHER CAR

12. For reflexive pronouns (MYSELF, YOURSELF, THEMSELVES, etc.), read ASL Notes #1 and #2 for details. Also, find out about adding intensity to the reflexive pronouns.

   a) Reflexive pronouns can function as the verb "To Be":

   English: I am a teacher.

   ASL: I MYSELF TEACHER.

   b) Reflexive pronouns also regularly function as nouns or pronouns:

   English: He is hearing.

   ASL: HIMSELF HEARING.

   c) For command or in anger:

   English: Clean up the garage yourself!

   ASL: CLEAN-UP GARAGE YOURSELF! (firm one-time movement)

13. Some adjectives can be moved either once or repeatedly. They are moved once if they are placed before a noun. Ex: MORE TIME, RED CAR.

14. Articles refer to "a," "an," "the" and "some." ASL does not use the indefinite articles "a" or "an."

"The" may be kept as a specifier in the environment of something that can be seen: I SEE POINT (the) CAR. (Substitute POINT for "the.") Delete "the" if the object cannot be seen or it is in an abstract form: I DON'T LIKE (the) WEATHER.

"Some" is used the same as in English: We need some food and some water. (Some ASL experts say "some" does not belong in ASL.)

15. Compare four different forms of comparative ASL adjectives

English: A gorilla is larger than a monkey.

ASL: a) GORILLA LARGER THAN MONKEY.

   b) GORILLA MORE LARGE THAN MONKEY.

   c) FOR BODY SIZE, GORILLA BEAT (shot-H) MONKEY.

   d) ------------T------------   ------------T-------------
      GORILLA [ix L], MONKEY [ix R]; LARGER, POINT [ix L].

16. Again on reflexive pronouns for a different use – as the verb "To Be."

English: Larry is a cop; I am a preacher.

ASL: LARRY HIMSELF COP; I MYSELF PREACHER/MYSELF PREACHER.

17. There are five kinds of auxiliary (helping) verbs:

   a) "To Be"

   b) "To Have"

   c) "To Do"

   d) modals

   e) "Used To"

18. Know the verbs that can be used for full directionality: TELL, SHOW, GIVE, etc.

Also identify the verbs that can be partially directional: COME, GO, READ, etc.

Find out which verbs cannot be directional: DRINK, THINK, WANT, SAY, etc.

19. Active Voice ~ Passive Voice: like English, ASL uses primarily <u>active</u> voice. Passive voice is allowed in a few situations:

    a) BUILD BY

    b) MAKE BY

    c) WRITE BY ("BY" is fingerspelled in all three situations.)

<u>Active voice</u> means the subject of the sentence is performing an action (the verb) upon something/someone (the direct object of the verb).

    <u>English</u>: ASL students watch many DVDs. (S Vt DO)

    <u>ASL</u>: ASL STUDENT WATCH MANY DVD.

In English <u>passive voice</u>, the direct object comes into subject position, the verb keeps the same tense but adds the appropriate tense of "To Be" plus the past participle (-ed/-en), and the subject becomes the object of the preposition "by," or disappears altogether.

    <u>English</u>: Many DVDs are watched (by ASL students).

20. <u>English</u>: The police caught the thief. (<u>active</u> voice, S Vt DO)

    <u>ASL</u>: 1) COP PAST CATCH THIEF. (S Vt DO)
            ----T----
        2) THIEF, COP FINISH CATCH. (DO S Vt) (not used in English)

    <u>English</u>: The thief <u>was caught</u> (by the police). (<u>passive</u> voice)

    <u>English</u>: The log cabin <u>was built</u> by a settler family. (<u>passive</u> voice)

    <u>ASL</u>: WOOD CABIN [fs] PAST <u>BUILD</u> BY [fs] SETTLER [fs] FAMILY.

178

KEY FOR INTERMEDIATE LEVEL STUDY QUESTIONS
Part B

1. "Won't." This term has two uses: One is for <u>not being able to</u>. In this case, you sign NOT or CAN'T but mouth "won't," shake head and furrow the eyebrows:

English: I <u>won't</u> meet you today.

ASL: I-MEET-YOU TODAY <u>NOT/CAN'T</u>.

The other use is for "refuse." Again, this term has two English meanings: The noun means "trash"; the verb means "choosing <u>not</u> to do something":

English: I <u>refuse</u> to take out the <u>refuse</u>.

ASL: I <u>REFUSE</u> THROW-OUT TRASH. (firm, but not negative, facial expression)

2. Examples of negative prefixes:

a) <u>Dis</u>: <u>dis</u>like, <u>dis</u>agree; sign NOT

b) <u>Un</u>: <u>un</u>satisfied, <u>un</u>wanted, <u>un</u>important; sign NOT

c) <u>Mis</u>: <u>mis</u>informed, <u>mis</u>interpret, <u>mis</u>take/<u>mis</u>took; sign WRONG

3. The placement of frequency words is anywhere in the sentence:

a) I <u>OFTEN</u> GO

b) I GO <u>OFTEN</u>

c) <u>OFTEN</u> GO I (Remember <u>not</u> to mouth "I" after the verb.)

d) I <u>OFTEN</u> GO <u>OFTEN</u>.

4. There are two important things to remember about time indicators:

a) Raise eyebrows.

b) Place the time concept up front–to provide the sense of time/tense.

(<u>Note</u>: This is for a one-time event, not for frequency.)

5. Preposition changes for day, week, month, year:

a) Day:

English: See you on Monday.　　　　ASL: SEE YOU FUTURE MONDAY.

b) Week:

English: We will meet in two weeks.　　ASL: NEXT-TWO-WEEK WE MEET.

c) Month:

English: in March　　　　　　　　ASL: LAST MARCH, NOW/THIS MARCH

English: next March　　　　　　　ASL: FUTURE MARCH

English: in three months　　　　　ASL: NEXT THREE-MONTH

d) Year:

English: 1) in 1975　　　　　　　ASL: 1) YEAR/PAST 1975
　　　　 2) in 2020　　　　　　　　　 2) FUTURE 2020

English: in five years　　　　　　ASL: 1) FIVE-YEAR-FROM-NOW
　　　　　　　　　　　　　　　　　　　 2) FUTURE FIVE YEAR

6. The prepositions "from," "to" and "during" function very similarly in both English and ASL.

"On" and "in," however, do not. Whereas these two prepositions function idiomatically in English ("See you on the first Tuesday in August"), they are much more literal in ASL, meaning "on top of" and "inside of," respectively.

"In" is used in ASL only for something with a cover: IN WATER, IN CAR, IN CUP. "I live in Las Vegas" is signed I LIVE LV or I LIVE THERE LV.

The preposition "of" is used rarely in ASL, except for proper names: "The Johnson family of Chicago" is signed JOHNSON [fs] FAMILY FROM CHICAGO.

7. The primary purpose for using prepositions in ASL is location: UNDER TABLE, NEXT-TO TABLE, ON (top of) TABLE.

8. Four coordinating conjunctions:

    a) "and"

    b) "but"

    c) "or/#OR"

    d) "nor" (this is signed not in ASL)

9. Five substitutions for "and":

    a) PLUS: BROTHER PLUS SISTER

    b) BOTH: BOTH APPLE, ORANGE

    c) ALSO: DOG ALSO CAT

    d) Ranking (point on non-dominant finger): 1) RED, 2) BLUE, 3) YELLOW

    e) Shoulder shift: MOTHER-R, FATHER-L

10. Four correlative conjunctions:

    a) **"Both. . . and. . ."**:

        English: = both mother and father

        ASL: BOTH MOTHER, FATHER

    b) **"Not only. . . but also. . ."**:

        English: not only you but also your sister

        ASL: YOU, ALSO YOUR SISTER

   c) **"<u>Either</u>. . . <u>or</u>. . .":**

      <u>English</u>: <u>either</u> you <u>or</u> your brother

      ASL: YOU <u>OR</u> YOUR BROTHER

   d) **"<u>Neither</u>. . . <u>nor</u>. . .":**

      <u>English</u>: neither Bob <u>nor</u> Bill

      <u>ASL</u>: 1) <u>NOT</u> BOB [fs], <u>NOT</u> BILL [fs];
           2) BOB [fs], BILL [fs] <u>NOT</u>

11. Interjections are expressions used to exclaim, protest or command. For accurate signing: Exaggerate facial expression and body language for intensity and increase speed of the sign.

   a) I GOT #JOB!

   b) GOOD!

   c) WE WANT DISCOUNT!

   d) AWESOME!

   e) YUCK!

   f) STOP-IT!

12. "There is"/"there are" is an idiomatic English expression. ASL signs HAVE.

   <u>English</u>: <u>There is</u> a car show on Saturday.

   <u>ASL</u>: THIS SATURDAY <u>HAVE</u> CAR SHOW.

   <u>English</u>: <u>There was</u> a lizard on the window.

   <u>ASL</u>: WINDOW FINISH <u>HAVE</u> LIZARD [fs].

13. For a topic marker, do two things:

I) Place the main idea up front.

2) Raise eyebrows only for the idea, followed by normal eyebrows for supporting details.

```
                 -----------------T-----------------
```
ASL: <u>PALOMAR COLLEGE</u> HAVE 30,000 STUDENT.

14. There is a marked difference between Q and WQ:

<u>Q</u> = asking questions for an answer of either <u>yes</u>, <u>no</u> or <u>maybe</u>:

```
       --------------------Q--------------------
```
YOU HAVE TIME NOW?

<u>WQ</u> = asking questions for information or answers other than yes and no:

```
         -------------------------WQ--------------------
```
WHAT KIND CAR YOU LIKE?

15. <u>English</u>: Do you like Hawaii?

```
           -----------------Q--------------
```
ASL: YOU LIKE HAWAII? (full-length Q)

You can save Q for last if you pose a long Yes/No question:

<u>English</u>: Do you want me to go back to the house and check to make sure the stove has been turned off?

ASL: I GO-BACK HOUSE CHECK MAKE SURE STOVE FINISH TURN-OFF,
```
         -----------Q---------
```
YOU WANT?

16. Whereas WQ interrogative question words (WHO? WHERE? WHY? HOW?, etc.) expect an answer from the listener/receiver, the same words used in a RQ alert the listener/receiver that the speaker/signer will give the answer immediately.

<u>English</u>: The class is going to Sea World.

```
         ---RQ---
```
ASL: Class go where? Sea World.

English: Nebraska Huskers fans wear red and white clothing for home games.

ASL: HOME GAME NEB HUSKERS [fs] SUPPORTER WEAR
------------RQ------------
WHAT COLOR? RED, WHITE.

------------------------WQ------------------------
17. WQ = WHEN GALLAUDET ESTABLISH? (looking for a factual answer)

---RQ---
RQ = GALLAUDET ESTABLISH WHEN? 1864. (asking then answering immediately)

18. The key words for an ASL conditional clause are: IF, WHEN/HAPPEN, AFTER, BEFORE, SINCE, WHILE.

Place the CC up front, plus, raise eyebrows (only for the CC part):

--------------CC--------------------
AFTER WE GO CLASS, WE GO HOME.

----------------------------CC--------------------------
WHEN SPRING SEMESTER FINISH, SUMMER BREAK START.

19. Unlike in English, "thousand" is not articulated or signed for the years of the 21st century. They are fingerspelled 2-0-0-0 or 20-20 (1x, 1x), etc.

20. There are no name signs for the months of the year. Instead, abbreviated words are fingerspelled for each, no periods. If the name is short, it is spelled out in full:

JAN, FEB, MARCH, APRIL, MAY, JUNE, JULY, AUG, SEPT, OCT, NOV, DEC

21. There are approximately 85 fingerspelled loan signs, such as #JOB, #EARLY, #CLUB, etc. They are glossed with the number sign [#] to differentiate them from regular signs and regular fingerspelling: YES ~ #YES. Pick any four from the full list of fingerspelled loan signs in this Handbook, for example: #BUSY, #COOL, #FAV, #WOW.

22. Memorize only the first six pages. Your instructor will select an English phrase which you will translate into its ASL equivalent; for example:

English:	ASL:
The Fourth of July	JULY 4th
Already	FINISH
Book fair	BOOK SALE

KEY FOR ADVANCED LEVEL STUDY QUESTIONS
Part A

1. Parts of speech with ending markers:

   <u>English</u>:

   a) noun (flower<u>s</u>, glass<u>es</u>, ox<u>en</u>)

   b) adjective (interest<u>ing</u>, bor<u>ed</u>, fret<u>ful</u>, happi<u>est</u>)

   c) verb (sing<u>s</u>, play<u>ed</u>, throw<u>ing</u>)

   d) adverb (slow<u>ly</u>, fast<u>er</u>)

   <u>ASL</u>:

   a) certain nouns (BILL<u>S</u>, MIL<u>ES</u>, HOUR<u>S</u>)

   b) certain adjectives (SMART<u>ER</u>, TALL<u>EST</u>)

   c) certain adverbs (SLOW<u>ER</u>, FAST<u>EST</u>)

2. The following verb types are nonexistent in ASL:

   a) "To Be" (am, is, are, was, were, being, been)

   b) infinitives (<u>to</u> talk, <u>to</u> run, etc.)

   c) Verb contractions (he<u>'d</u>, is<u>n't</u>, she<u>'ll</u>, we<u>'re</u>, could<u>n't</u>, etc.)

3. Normally time indicators are placed at the beginning of a sentence to set up the verb tense. However, if the sentence is short, the time indicator can be placed at the end:

   SEE YOU <u>MONDAY</u>.

   HAVE EXAM <u>NEXT-TWO-WEEK</u>.

4. The following are examples of ASL structures without English "and":

   a) BLACK, WHITE TV

   b) 5½

c) SHORT, SWEET

d) See other examples in this *Handbook*.

5. Below are examples of English and ASL correlative conjunction usage:

a) Both ... and ...

English	ASL
<u>Both</u> deaf <u>and</u> hard of hearing . . .	1) DEAF, HARD-OF-HEARING . . . 2) BOTH DEAF, HARD-OF-HEARING . . .

b) Not only ... but also ...

English	ASL
<u>Not only</u> coffee, <u>but also</u> tea . . .	1) COFFEE <u>PLUS</u> TEA . . . 2) <u>BOTH</u> COFFEE, TEA . . .

c) Either . . . or . . .

English	ASL
<u>Either</u> Tom <u>or</u> Bob . . .	1) TOM [fs] #<u>OR</u> BOB [fs] . . . 2) TOM [fs], BOB [fs] <u>EITHER</u> . . .

d) <u>Neither . . . nor . . .</u>

English	ASL
<u>Neither</u> you <u>nor</u> I . . .	1) <u>NOT</u> YOU, <u>NOT</u> I . . . 2) <u>BOTH</u> YOU, I <u>NOT</u> . . .

6. ASL prepositions are generally used for <u>location</u>:

a) <u>UNDER</u> CHAIR

b) <u>NEXT</u> TV

c) <u>OVER</u> FENCE

d) <u>ACROSS</u> PARK

e) <u>NEAR</u> 7-11 STORE

7. Wh- questions can become Yes/No questions.

<u>ASL Examples</u>:

----------Q--------------
WHERE PUPPY? (excitement)

--------------------Q----------------------------
WHO WON WORLD SERIES? (curiosity)

----------------Q----------------------------
WHY NOT WE GO BEACH? (anticipation)

-------Q------------
HOW YOU? (conversation starter)

8. How do ASL tag questions differ from English tag questions?

Both ASL and English use tag questions, but English is much more complex in its structure. ASL simply uses RIGHT? TRUE? or HUH? (wiggled index finger)

<u>ASL examples</u>:

----Q----
a) MEET-YOU BOOKSTORE, <u>RIGHT</u>?

----Q---
b) OUR EXAM POSTPONE, <u>TRUE</u>?

---Q---
c) YOU GOT GRADE-A, <u>HUH</u>?

9. When is an ASL adverbial time clause put at the end of a sentence?

When a sentence contains a time sensitive sequence, place the adverbial clause toward the end of the sentence. Do <u>not</u> raise eyebrows for this placement of a conditional clause.

<u>ASL examples</u>:

a) BERTIE [fs], TOMMIE [fs] TEACH FOR 35 YEAR <u>BEFORE THEY RETIRE</u>.

b) I MUST STUDY++ <u>UNTIL I KNOW ALL INFORMATION</u>.

c) PLEASE WAIT FOR ME <u>IF CAN</u>.

10. When does one fingerspell in a circle?

Fingerspelling goes in a circle to indicate a person's middle initial and for U.S./U.S.A.

<u>ASL examples</u>:

a) MAN NAME JOHN [fs] F. (fs in a circle) KENNEDY [fs] PRESIDENT FROM 1961-1963.

b) NORTH AMERICA HAVE THREE COUNTRY: 1) CANADA, 2) U. S. (fs in a circle), 3) MEXICO.

11. The following expressions are used with the fingerspelled IT:

a) DO <u>IT</u>.

b) FORGET <u>IT</u>.

c) GO FOR <u>IT</u>.

d) LOVE <u>IT</u>.

e) MAKE <u>IT</u>.

f) THAT('s) <u>IT</u>.

g) WORTH <u>IT</u>.

12. Below are some English phrases where "it" is <u>not</u> expressed in the ASL translation:

<u>English</u>	<u>ASL</u>
a) Take <u>it</u> easy.	a) TAKE-EASY.
b) <u>It</u> is important to study.	b) IMPORTANT STUDY.
c) I'll take care of <u>it</u>.	c) I WILL TAKE-CARE-OF.

13. What are the corresponding ASL translations of the following English prefixes?

English	ASL
"dis-" = "not"; "<u>dis</u>pleasure"	<u>NOT</u> PLEASURE
"en-" = "make"; <u>en</u>able	MAKE ABLE
"ex-" = "former"; "<u>ex</u>-teacher"	#EX TEACHER
"il-" = "not"; "<u>il</u>legal"	<u>NOT</u> LEGAL or FORBID
"im-" = "not; "<u>im</u>perfect"	<u>NOT</u> PERFECT
"un" = "not"; "<u>un</u>happy:	<u>NOT</u> HAPPY

14. Numbers 1-5 are fingerspelled up front for specific purposes, including:

a) age

b) time

c) address

d) telephone numbers

e) room numbers

f) course numbers (ASL IV, Spanish III, e.g.)

15. Distinguished from regular fingerspelling, loan signs involve some kind of modification involving one or more of the following:

a) deleted letters

b) change in palm orientation, location, movement

c) circled, twisted, snapped or sliding hand movement

d) directional movement

16. The rule of thumb for frequency of RQ by skilled signers is once every 25-50 sentences.

KEY FOR ADVANCED LEVEL STUDY QUESTIONS
Part B

1. Examples of intensifiers in ASL include: LESS, MORE, MOST, TOO, A-LITTLE.

2. English relative pronouns include: who/whom, whose, that, which and whose for noun and adjective clauses. ASL does not have "which" or "whom," and signs WHO'S for "whose." For adverb clauses, English uses because, when(ever) and where(ever). ASL does not use the (ever) form; it also avoids "because," preferring the RQ form of the sentence.

   <u>ASL Examples:</u>

   a) I KNOW <u>WHO</u> WORK IN OFFICE. (S of DO Cl)

   b) YOUR FRIEND SAW YOU <u>WHERE</u> YOU BUY FLOWER. (Adv Cl)

3. a) <u>Transitive:</u> I <u>KICK</u> BALL. (Vt transfers the action from subject to object.)

    b) <u>Intransitive:</u> EAGLE <u>FLY</u>. (No direct object of the verb)

    c) <u>Linking:</u> (1) <u>APPEAR</u>, <u>FEEL</u>, <u>LOOK</u>, <u>SMELL</u>, <u>TASTE</u>, <u>SEEM</u> (sensory verbs):

      I <u>LOOK</u> AND <u>FEEL</u> GOOD.

      (2) "To Become": SICK DOG <u>BECOME</u> BETTER.

      (3) "To Be" replaced by a reflexive pronoun: <u>MYSELF</u> DEAF.

      (4) "To Be" replaced by PAST, PRESENT, FUTURE: SHE <u>FUTURE</u> COP.

4. One exception for "To Be" in ASL is CAN'T BE [fs].

5. Start with the largest time concept and end with the smallest one:

   -----------------------------TI----------------------------------
   <u>ASL Example:</u> <u>LAST-YEAR</u>, <u>MARCH 10</u>, <u>TIME 7 NIGHT</u> . . .

6. Generally, ASL uses prepositions only for location; English prepositions are either deleted or replaced.

English	ASL
Class of 2015	CLASS 2015
See you on Tuesday.	SEE YOU TUESDAY.
We will meet again in June.	WE MEET AGAIN NEXT JUNE.
The farmers are picking apples off the trees.	FARMER PICK APPLE FROM TREE++.

7. ASL verbs that utilize head-nodding include: AGREE, CAN, LIKE, KNOW, UNDERSTAND, WANT.

8. Wh- words that can be fingerspelled for a one-word question include: HOW, WHEN, WHERE, WHO, WHY.

9. One-word fingerspelled Wh- words are appropriate for expressing the following:

   a) anger

   b) curiosity

   c) surprise

   d) demanding an answer

10. Two subordinating adverbs have questionable usage in formal ASL:

   a) "because" (Change to RQ "WHY?")

   b) "unless" (Change to IF NOT.)

11. a) Movement (speed, direction)

   b) Location (NEAR, FAR, LEFT, RIGHT, FRONT, BACK, etc.)

   c) Palm orientation/set-up

d) Indication of how many/how much

e) Shape and size

12. Do not use "AND" between verbs:

English	ASL
We always study <u>and</u> eat at the same time.	WE ALWAYS STUDY, EAT SAME TIME. (delete "AND")

Also, do not use "AND" for <u>three or more</u> nouns or adjectives. "AND" can be replaced by "PLUS."

English	ASL
I need to buy lettuce, tomatoes <u>and</u> carrots.	I NEED BUY 1) LETTUCE, 2) TOMATO, 3) CARROT.
The beach house is small, cute, <u>and</u> pricey.	BEACH HOUSE SMALL, CUTE <u>PLUS</u> EXPENSIVE.

13. "WILL" is not signed if the tense of the sentence or conversation is already in future mode, having been established earlier with "NEXT WEEK," or "NOW/THIS AFTERNOON," etc.

14. The three ways to translate the English word "of" into ASL include:

a) Simply delete "of": "Class of 2020" becomes CLASS 2020.

b) Replace "of" with "FROM": "The Smythes of New York" becomes: SMYTHE [fs] FAMILY <u>FROM</u> NEW-YORK.

c) Fingerspell "OF" for titles or other proper nouns: NATIONAL ASSOCIATION <u>OF</u> [fs] THE [fs] DEAF.

15. Below are the key signs for sensory verbs, a type of linking verb:

a) APPEAR/SEEM (-LIKE)

b) FEEL (-LIKE)

c) LOOK-LIKE

d) SMELL (-LIKE)

e) SOUND-LIKE

f) TASTE (-LIKE)

16. There are only three number systems that can incorporate 10 imbedded into the Rule of 9:

a) age

b) dollars, cents

c) minutes

17. The abbreviated fingerspelled months are:

a) JAN

b) FEB

c) AUG

d) SEPT (4 letters)

e) OCT

f) NOV

g) DEC

18. The three reasons for using a double pronoun are:

a) emphasis   Ex: I WANT GO <u>I</u>.

b) personal style   Ex: HE HEARING <u>HE</u>.

c) variety   Ex: YOU PASS <u>YOU</u>.

(<u>Note</u>: Remember NOT to mouth the double pronoun at the end.)

19. Sign HAPPEN for ONCE:

English	ASL
	-----------------CC--------------
<u>Once</u> the rain has stopped, the birds will sing again.	<u>HAPPEN</u> RAIN STOP, BIRD SING AGAIN.

20. Do not mouth /cha/ for something bigger, taller or longer. Instead, mouth "bigger," "taller" or "longer." One could also mouth "more big," "more tall" or "more long." Or one could mouth nothing at all.

FROM YOUR AUTHORS

In my infancy, I was diagnosed with profound deafness in both ears by the Naval Hospital at Balboa Park in San Diego. My parents soon found help from the world-famous John Tracy Clinic in Los Angeles, which has encouraged parents to raise their deaf children without depending on sign language for communication. With hearing amplification and speech training, I struggled to communicate and gain a stronghold on English. My mother spent a lot of time daily teaching me to lipread and sight read. I also learned to write my name, the numbers and some words. Despite my mother's dedication and my efforts, the aural-oral approach was not a perfect fit for me.

In the fall of 1964, I learned American Sign Language at the Missouri School for the Deaf at Fulton (MSD). For the first time in the seven years of my young life, I felt complete because I could finally understand and participate in human two-way communication. Later, at the California School for the Deaf at Riverside (CSDR), I mastered ASL. As is true for any deaf student, I struggled to learn English, but my teachers never gave up. With their patience, I learned the aural-oral English language little by little, finally gaining a comfortable command of the language by using the Fitzgerald Key, a popular method for teaching the deaf nationwide from the 1930s to the 1980s, and by investing my free time in vocabulary studies and leisure reading, including 300 books for pleasure during my last three years of high school.

This *American Sign Language ~ English Comparative Linguistics Handbook* is a reminder of my developmental years with language at MSD and CSDR—learning a language by analyzing its patterns of vocabulary, syntax and semantics (the "rules of grammar")—accompanied by examples and subsequent drill. Many language teachers today view this methodology as outdated, embracing instead the "whole language" theory: using the target language in reading, writing and group activities. This modern approach has merit, but the original step-by-step language analysis approach works well, too. In my more than thirty years of ASL teaching experience, I have seen again and again how my approach has helped students gain a stronger command of ASL and, in the process, a deeper appreciation of their own native English language, as many of them never had a formal opportunity to study their language in depth. Dr. Ginger—my writing colleague with forty years of experience teaching both English and English to Speakers of Other Languages (ESOL) and more than ten years of teaching ASL, plus ESOL to deaf students using ASL—shares my philosophy for teaching ASL, English and ESOL with this effective, "old-fashioned" methodology.

I am grateful to my dear late mother, MSD and CSDR for introducing me to human communication and for enriching my experience with the two languages that I have come to understand well and use effortlessly.

Kevin Struxness

As far back as I can remember I wanted to become a teacher; I recall as a toddler teaching everything I learned to anyone who would listen. Studying ballet as a youngster, I fell in love with French dance terms and wondered what it would be like for little French girls to learn English—hence my inspiration for teaching English to Speakers of Other Languages, my master's degree major. I adored the structure of my own English language as soon as I became aware of it. One student teacher visiting my seventh grade English class whispered to his colleague, "What the heck are correlative conjunctions?" "Never heard of 'em," replied the other young man. Not one to miss an opportunity to teach, I whispered, "They are conjunctions that come in pairs: 'either-or,' 'neither-nor,' 'both-and,' 'not only-but also.'" When I found myself continually frustrated by my tenth grade English teacher's poor spelling and grammar, I made the grand life decision to become a high school English teacher so that the students could have a good role model. I have now taught English and ESOL at all levels for more than four decades, and somehow remain passionate about it!

Those many years of grading student themes and research papers qualified me to become a professional editor, copyeditor and proofreader. While teaching ESOL in Honolulu more than a decade ago, and editing on the side, I managed to take an adult education summer school class in American Sign Language—and within five minutes I knew that I had to become an interpreter and teacher of this extraordinarily beautiful and complicated language! I transferred to Kapi`olani Community College, finished ASL and entered the interpreting program. After a year of interpreting studies, I moved back to North County San Diego and transferred to Palomar College, where I graduated from the ASL/English Interpreter Training Program in 2003. Prof. Kevin Struxness was my first instructor. Shortly thereafter he invited me to copyedit and proofread his history book on the California School for the Deaf at Riverside. When my part of the project had finished, he asked if I would like to collaborate with him on this *Handbook*, which he has been formulating over the many years of his ASL teaching career.

I am honored to have the opportunity to share with my ASL students, and others, what I hope is a focused bird's-eye view of some of the structure and patterns of their own exquisite auditory-verbal English language and some of the many ways that it compares and contrasts with the beautiful visual-spatial patterns of American Sign Language.

Ginger Marable